SUPERPARENTING!

also by Dr Amber Elliott

Why Can't My Child Behave?
Empathic Parenting Strategies That Work for Adoptive and Foster Families
Dr Amber Elliott
ISBN 978 1 84905 339 6
eISBN 978 0 85700 671 4

SUPER
PARENTING!

BOOST YOUR THERAPEUTIC
PARENTING THROUGH TEN
TRANSFORMATIVE STEPS

Dr Amber Elliott

Foreword by Sally Donovan

Jessica Kingsley Publishers
London and Philadelphia

First published in Great Britain in 2021 by Jessica Kingsley Publishers
An Hachette Company

1

A CIP catalogue record for this title is available from the
British Library and the Library of Congress

ISBN 978 1 78592 095 0
eISBN 978 1 78450 357 4

Printed and bound in Great Britain by TJ Books Limited

Jessica Kingsley Publishers' policy is to use papers that are natural,
renewable and recyclable products and made from wood grown in
sustainable forests. The logging and manufacturing processes are expected
to conform to the environmental regulations of the country of origin.

Jessica Kingsley Publishers
Carmelite House
50 Victoria Embankment
London EC4Y 0DZ

www.jkp.com

MIX
Paper from
responsible sources
FSC® C013056

Contents

Foreword

SALLY DONOVAN

When a developmentally traumatized child comes into our lives with their precious few possessions and their certain belief that they are not secure in their world, we have a job on our hands to begin building a trusting and lasting relationship with them.

It might not be too long before we realize that almost everything we thought we knew about child–parent relationships is wrong. The basic rules of how things are done, how folk cooperate with each other and who calls the shots get torn up (and quite possibly thrown in our faces). Our first response is usually to try harder – to parent harder, louder, tougher. And it doesn't help. Mostly it makes things worse. It's like charging at a locked door with our fists, when what we need is a key.

We learn about the special kind of parenting our children need – therapeutic parenting – and we make our first tentative steps at introducing it into our repertoire. Its approach and methods make sense and seem kind of straightforward, until, that is, we actually have to carry it out with a child who is stuck deep in their trauma.

In this book Dr Amber Elliot refers to the kind of parenting that foster carers, kinship carers and adopters carry out as 'superparenting', and it is just that. It is way more demanding than the average, 'what everyone else is doing' type of parenting. The knowledge, practice, thought and finesse required to navigate our way through the day, the week, the term, the year with a traumatized child is astonishing and frequently under-estimated. Therapeutic parenting is psychologically complex and at times overwhelming.

I've come to realize that the overriding reason why many of us find therapeutic parenting so difficult is not our child, but the cultural baggage associated with children and parenting that pervades our society. I'm talking about a particularly British style of cultural baggage here, which has seeped into our brains whether we live in the UK or a part of the world that has had 'British values' thrust upon it. When I was a child, you did what you were told, partly out of fear and partly out of a strong desire to 'be good' or to be seen to be so. You worked hard. You ate your vegetables. You didn't answer back. You certainly weren't encouraged to develop much in the way of critical thinking. And what you sometimes hear trotted out by the traditionalists, that in the good old days children respected authority – that bit isn't true. You complied with authority to keep out of trouble. Most of the time you despised it, particularly when you witnessed that the way it threw its power around was unfair and sometimes cruel. It created a huge gulf between children and adults. In therapeutic parenting, we're working to connect with children, to bring ourselves in closer, not to drive them even further away. This is why traditional methods can fail so spectacularly. That's why we can find ourselves pounding on locked doors until our knuckles are bruised, screaming 'Why can't you just do what I tell you to do?'

Amber's first book, *Why Can't My Child Behave?*, hit this spot perfectly and resonated with its many readers. In this, her second book, she gives us permission to understand and accept our parenting impulses and to appreciate their power over us. She does this with real heart and without a shred of blame. Amber is one of those professionals we all hope to have in our lives – she has an immense amount of knowledge and experience of child development and trauma *and* she gets it. If you are a therapeutic parent, you will instantly know what I mean by that. 'Getting it' is shorthand for not having to explain or justify yourself.

Superparenting! sets out why we bounce back into old habits when we are under strain and the ways we can build in opportunities to re-centre ourselves. Amber includes lots of useful, everyday scenarios, many of which will be familiar to readers. I spotted myself a few times (hello 'Yolanda'). The scenarios are presented in a way that doesn't make you feel as if you're failing. They are always a jumping-off point for taking new and hopeful perspectives. And then we are offered a choice of tools to fit the many different situations we find ourselves in.

We are all of us doing our imperfect best for our traumatized children, and *Superparenting!* meets us where we are with heart, hope and encouragement. We need plenty of all of these when we're walking alongside a child, building a real and long-lasting connection, especially when we are fending off the authoritarians whilst we're doing it. Building a connection is impossible when we are either side of a locked door. What *Superparenting!* does really well is hand us the keys to unlock meaningful connections with our children so we may build relationships based on the firm foundations of trust and safety.

Sally Donovan, author of *The Unofficial Guide to
Therapeutic Parenting – The Teen Years*

Note from the Author

How to use this book

I wanted to write a little guide to using this book – because it *is* a book to be used, a reference really, rather than something to be read cover to cover in the expectation that you'll absorb it in its entirety.

Trying to parent children when they are showing you their trauma-triggered behaviours is tough, and none of us are perfect. *Superparenting!* is an attempt to acknowledge the superhuman lengths that trauma-parents (parents and carers of traumatized children) go to, and the heroic strength it takes to be empathic in the face of challenge, resistance and sometimes even aggression. It is also a nod towards our 'superkids' – these fantastic people who have survived their trauma, getting through childhoods that many of us would struggle to even imagine.

Superparenting! is most certainly not a book that will provide you with perfect ideas. I don't have all the answers, at least, not all the right ones, not the perfect ones for you and your child at every given point in time. So, on that basis, this book can't possibly exist to tell you that anything you're doing is wrong. It might make you reflect and even cause you to change tack, but you must not allow yourself to engage with the mistaken idea that if you like the ideas in this book, then it means you've previously done parenting wrong in some way. We're broadly anti-shame here, so please let yourself off that particular hook.

There's a quote from Ann Voskamp that I love: 'Shame dies when stories are told in safe places.' My dearest hope is for this book to be somewhere safe for you, where you can leave your shame at the door and take from it what you need.

I hope this book will give you some ideas. However, if what you're doing works, then *please* keep doing it. Your job is too hard to throw away good ideas that are already working. You may, however, want to test the parenting strategies you are currently using against the following questions to see if they are preventing you from being therapeutic in your parenting.

A nuts and bolts checklist for superparenting

- Does your strategy only work for the short term? (Sometimes, though, that's better than nothing.)
- Does it work by creating fear?
- Does it work by creating shame?
- Does it work by recreating old, unhelpful (even abusive) patterns?
- Does it 'work' only in that it makes you briefly feel better, perhaps as though you have more control or influence? Or does it fleetingly give you a sense of justice?

If you answered with some yeses and you'd like to try something else, then sit back, relax, and prepare yourselves to get comfortable with emotions. Superparenting depends on emotions and emotional understanding. Your emotions and your empathy are the avenues into our children's inner worlds. If we observe and trust our feelings and those of our children, they will form the keys to transforming you into a therapeutic superparent and unlock new ways of parenting. Good luck!

Acknowledgements

To Tim, N and B who have joined me on my own imperfect super-parenting journey and from whom I've learnt so much. Tremendous thanks to Sally Ferris, without whom this book might have taken another 8 years. Also to Adele Freeman and Kim Golding, who supported and sense-checked along the way in the most honest and kindly of ways.

INTRODUCTION

Have you ever been in the situation of doing all the right things but not having the impact on your child that you want to? If so, you are not alone, and there's a very good reason for it.

The well-worn parenting advice based on reward–punishment thinking that we are all given is very often ineffective for children who have experienced trauma via abuse and/or neglect in their early lives. If you have faced rage outbursts, lying, stealing or a general inability to follow instructions and tackled them with reprimands, taking away screen time or descending into nagging, shouting and losing your cool without positive results, then **Empathic Behaviour Management (EBM)** might be worth a try (explained below; also see the Glossary).

What is reward–punishment thinking?

To be clear, this is not a book critiquing any specific parenting programme, largely because most parents and carers aren't really following one particular 'academic' way of doing things.

In this book we will explore and compare the parenting messages that parents and carers end up with from traditional approaches largely based on **behavioural and social learning theory-based programmes** (that advocate rewards, consequences, ignoring 'bad' behaviour and star charts, amongst other things).

These parenting messages are so ingrained as the 'right' way to parent that it can be difficult to work out what reward–punishment thinking is and what it isn't. So let's make it clear and easy.

In short, anything that encourages us to deal only with behaviour (and not feelings) using a reward or punishment/consequence of any kind has its roots in reward–punishment thinking. When we are on this parenting track it tends to permeate all of our thinking about how to interact with children. It can be as obvious as a star chart or grounding a child, or as subtle as busying yourself with something in order to ignore a child's 15th 'request' for a chocolate biscuit. All of these strategies require us to believe that in order to help our children we must train them using rewards and punishments.

It is important to understand, however, that many of these strategies can also make sense when coming from a therapeutic parenting or EBM point of view. Crucially, however, a different logic (approach) is necessary to ensure that children's emotional needs and drives are understood and accommodated as well as managing their challenging behaviours.

Common reward–punishment strategies include:

- Time out.
- Star charts.
- Grounding.
- Ignoring.
- Leaving children to cry.
- Praise.
- Using a cross face to communicate that you don't like a behaviour.
- Stickers for good behaviour or for being brave.

Again, please don't be panicked by this list. It's not that all of these strategies necessarily need to be abandoned, but typically we use them hoping to train the behaviour out of a child without consideration of the emotional drive that caused the behaviour in the first place.

Where do reward–punishment (traditional parenting) strategies come from?

What comes to mind when you think of a parenting 'strategy'? Are you thinking of star charts or time out, maybe even praise, grounding or taking away pocket money? All of these require us to use rewards and punishments.

To understand why reward–punishment thinking is so embedded in what we hear about parenting it's useful to look back and understand the science it came from. Whilst neither rewards nor punishments were 'invented' by anyone in particular, the work explored below is what formalized them as an integral part of 'good' parenting.

Burrhus Skinner[1, 2, 3] researched and popularized the use of rewards (reinforcers) and consequences (punishments) to shape and modify the behaviour of animals and humans. He had far-reaching ambitions for his ideas as ways of organizing society as a whole, writing about the drawbacks of free will and advocating for the use of rewards and consequences to shape and modify behaviour in populations at a political level.

In laboratory experiments Skinner was very successful in shaping the behaviour of animals; for example, he successfully taught rats to press levers to get food and, as every good psychology undergraduate knows, he even trained pigeons to play table tennis.[4]

In one of his more explicit forays into the world of parenting, Skinner tried to mechanize the care of babies via his 'air-crib' (or 'baby box'). He used it to control the conditions in which his second daughter was raised so that (he theorized) she would have no need to cry. Skinner was clear in his view that love and affection in relationships were limited in their impact to their use as rewards.

However, even Skinner went on, in his early 40s, to acknowledge the limited scientific understanding of the impact of love on children at that time: 'We are only just beginning to understand the power of love because we are just beginning to understand the weakness of force and aggression.'[5]

Skinner was not concerned with what went on inside the 'black box' of the human mind. Thanks to advances in **neuropsychology**, however, we can now explore and measure the impact of parenting and loving, affectionate relationships on our brains. We now know that relationships, particularly parent–child relationships, have an enormous impact on human brains. We also know that the brains of children who have experienced abuse and/or neglect can operate differently to the brains of those who haven't. This is an enormously exciting evolution of the science of relationships and parenting, and one I'm sure would have captivated Skinner and undoubtedly influenced his future work if he were around to see it.

Skinner's old-fashioned, reward–punishment legacy has clung on in our narratives of parenting to such a degree that it is still the default, go-to parenting approach, even in the face of new and better evidence.[6,7]

The one-size-fits-all model of training children and very deliberately ignoring their inner worlds is well overdue for a rethink. In the case of children traumatized by early abuse and/or neglect, the need for a new approach is crucial and urgent. In the next section we will explore in detail why we need to do this.

Why do we need an alternative?

First, and most fundamentally, there are some universal drawbacks to using reward–punishment thinking in parenting that are particularly relevant for children traumatized by abuse and/or neglect.

Let's take the issue of **countercontrol** first. The delivery of rewards and punishments requires control. When a relationship is dominated by control, the control tends to flip-flop both ways: are you rewarding your child with a star on their star chart for tidying their room, or are they tidying their room to make sure you give them a star for their star chart?

This can become more acute with children who don't have a fundamental trust in adults and whose relationships have become necessarily strategic and controlling as a result of earlier abuse and/ or maltreatment. Many parents and carers talk about countercontrol in terms of feeling manipulated and controlled by their children, particularly when children learn to achieve what they want by following the rules and then reverting to their default ways of being. Reward–punishment thinking often teaches children how to get around the rules but can fail to teach positive ways of relating and behaving. The emotional effect of this for parents and carers means that they often abandon the strategy or become increasingly punitive and focus instead on getting control back: 'You can't have a reward. You should tidy your room anyway.'

Another factor involves the abundance of desired things (reinforcers or rewards). In order for rewards to be effective, children must live in an environment in which the rewards we give are not readily available, that is, holding back some of the things children want most. In the case of chocolate and other material things this may not necessarily feel like too much of a drawback, as these are often the things that we try and give them only sparingly. However, the withdrawal of social interaction, comfort and play may be hugely counter-productive, and sometimes even damaging.

Since Skinner developed his theory, we now have greater scientific understanding of the impact of love and affection in relationships on our bodies, brains and emotional wellbeing, particularly that in parent–child and caregiving relationships.

We know that human infant brains are shaped by the love and care that they receive. It is not, as Skinner predicted, just that babies' behaviour is shaped by the reinforcement that love and affection provide for some behaviours. We have evidence that love and affection are crucial for healthy human functioning and not just emotional and mental health, and this also applies to physical health. Studies exploring Adverse Childhood Experiences (ACEs) (see below) show us that the more adverse experiences a person has in childhood (abuse, neglect, witnessing violence, etc.), the less safe a person feels; and the less sensitive, **attuned** (attentive and responsive), love and affection a person gets, the more likely they are to suffer with an enormous range of psychological and physical difficulties.[8] The practicalities of this are astounding. We know that early trauma can lead to increased risk of challenges that range from alcohol abuse issues through to autoimmune diseases and cancer. To illustrate this point, the Centers for Disease Control and Prevention (CDC) estimate that up to 1.9 million cases of heart disease and 21 million cases of depression in the USA could have been potentially avoided by preventing ACEs.[9]

Examples of high levels of ACEs impacting on psychological
and physical difficulties in adulthood[10, 11, 12]

Psychological difficulties	Physical difficulties
Alcoholism and alcohol abuse	Chronic obstructive pulmonary disease
Depression	Health-related quality of life
Drug use	Foetal death
Poor work performance	Ischemic heart disease
Financial stress	Liver disease
Risk for intimate partner violence	Sexually transmitted diseases
Smoking	Lung cancer
Suicide attempts	Frequent headaches
Unintended pregnancies	Autoimmune diseases

Unlike in Skinner's era, we know better now than to think that love and affection are merely ways of rewarding children's behaviour.

Beyond a shadow of scientific doubt, the sensitivity and **attunement** of affectionate loving relationships are integral to positive human functioning.[13] These are key ingredients in making a human work well, just like food and water.

So Skinner, whose reward–punishment parenting legacy lives on so potently, considerably underestimated the importance of love and affection in parenting, and the nuts and bolts of our parenting strategies have not moved far beyond these early strategies. On the surface level we react to our children's emotions and the behaviours they trigger by rewarding the emotional reaction we like and punishing (or withholding rewards for) the ones we don't.

We also apply this logic in a much less objective, analytical way when we feel emotionally triggered by a child's behaviour – we just find it intolerable, as I will go on to explain (these are post-hoc rationalizations, which are covered in Superpower #1: Parental Self-Acceptance).

Neurological evidence

Most of us think of our brains as fixed and unchangeable, like a computer. However, developments in neuroimaging since 2000 have proved that this is far from true.

Human brains are not complete, pre-formed, immutable objects. They are incredibly dynamic and adaptive entities that journey with us in our lives, moulding to our needs and shaping our capacity in the world.

Our brains do most of this adaptation in response to our environment before birth and in the first few years of life; indeed, they are at their most malleable at this early stage of life. This means that the incredible ability of our brains to develop to suit our social and physiological environment is maximized during this time. This process provides us with a neurological template for our understanding of ourselves, our relationships with others and the world. In short, our experiences as very young children provide us with our neurologically programmed expectations for the subsequent years. These templates can be changed later in our lives, but it is never quite as quick or easy as it is early in life.

However, there are two problems with this wonderful evolutionary process, which enables humans to adapt to and generalize from the environment in which they are born. The first is when our caregiving environment and relationships are very different from our other environments and secondary relationships, such as those we have in school, the workplace, etc. The second is when early life and later life require quite different templates. When the closest relationships in our early years are very different from our later experiences (such as adoptive or foster care), our template is all wrong. When our templates don't fit, our strategies for being and interacting don't fit...ultimately, *we* don't fit.

Although changes can most certainly be made later in childhood (and adulthood), changes at this stage are harder won. Children who have experienced abuse and/or neglect overwhelmingly have impaired executive function abilities (see below).[14, 15] In addition, a person who has experienced an early overdose of shame (shame is inherent in a prolonged experience of abuse and/or neglect) will be hypersensitive to the necessary (small doses of) shame integral to reward–punishment strategies (this is fully explored below).

So how does this help us to understand why we need to find an alternative to reward–punishment thinking for children traumatized by abuse and/or neglect? In short, because brains with a template for high stress and shame can struggle to either tolerate or regulate the stress and shame created by the rupture in relationship that reward–punishment thinking requires. Therefore, the combination of early trauma and reward–punishment thinking can be a recipe for **toxic stress**.

Toxic stress

Toxic stress is caused by the human body's stress management system being in use frequently or for prolonged periods of time. In young children this system activates when they are exposed to frightening, distressing or anxiety-provoking experiences. The effect of these experiences can be dramatically mediated by access to a sensitive, attuned adult who can help a child to make sense of challenging emotions and regulate them.[16] In situations of abuse and neglect, children not only have to deal with these frightening experiences; they also, very often, have no adult to help them with their consequent fears and anxieties.

The stress hormone, cortisol, is the neurochemical that is responsible for the damage done to brains in frequent or prolonged periods of stress. Cortisol is an extremely useful chemical when stress is infrequent and short-lived. It diverts our body's resources to areas that need to work well under stress. Short bursts of cortisol mobilize energy stores, enhance relevant types of memory and activate immune responses. However, long-term production of cortisol can cause suppression of memory and immune function, and contribute to physical health problems such as bone mineral loss and muscle atrophy, and even cause changes in the architecture of the brain regions associated with learning and memory.[17, 18, 19] As well as directly impacting on brain architecture (particularly the hippocampus), prolonged and/or frequent exposure to cortisol can also affect whether genes relevant to stress regulation are switched 'on' or 'off'.[20] These impacts of toxic stress have the potential to last a lifetime and do not change simply because a child changes caregiving environments.

Executive functions

This is the technical term for the most sophisticated neurological skills humans possess. As anyone who has had any contact with babies knows, we are not born with the ability to control our impulses, think about anyone else's feelings or plan our actions. However, we are born with the potential, in the pre-frontal cortex of our brain, to do all of these things. But that potential can only be realized in certain conducive environments.

Executive functions are developed most effectively in the early years via sensitive, attuned care. This process begins with adult acceptance of dependence and moves tiny step by tiny step towards independence in response to a child's ability to succeed in taking each of those steps. It requires caregivers to be emotionally and physically available, attuned and responsive to children's dependency needs and their gradually emerging capacity for independence.[21, 22, 23, 24, 25, 26, 27, 28] This very definitely does *not* mean pushing and cajoling a child (using rewards and punishments) to move to independence before their behaviour indicates that they are capable of it.

Executive functions are incredibly important to functioning throughout life. We know that these are the most crucial characteristics when it comes to school readiness and cognitive and social skills development. Whilst humans are born with innate intelligence, it is the development of the executive functions that allows us to use this intelligence in our day-to-day lives. These skills also profoundly impact children's abilities to form and maintain positive, mutually rewarding relationships in general, and parent–child relationships in particular.[29, 30, 31, 32]

When parenting children traumatized by abuse and/or neglect, our first task is to understand any limitations in their executive functions. Then we must meet them where they are and support their development to build up step by step (at their pace) from where they are rather than where we expect them to be based on their age.

We cannot get them there more quickly by treating them as if they have, or should have, the skills we might expect them to.[33]

Just as with a younger child, we need to make allowances for what traumatized children cannot do, but we also need to help them to make progress towards being able to do these things. For example, we would not expect a 2-year-old to concentrate on one task for 30 minutes. Similarly, sitting a 14-year-old, with significantly impaired attention, down to do the same is doomed to failure. It is highly likely to trigger increased levels of shame and despair alongside decreased levels of motivation, trust and cooperation. In the same way, none of us would expect an 18-month-old to be able to resist chasing their ball as it rolled into the road, and neither can we expect a 10-year-old with limited impulse control to have sufficient road sense to play outside safely without adult support.

Good results will come from putting in place the necessary support and awareness of when (and indeed, if) a child is able to move to the next level of responsibility. Simply doing it all at once because 'She's 12 years old, she has to learn!' will not help things to move forwards. The pressures on parents in this regard are huge; it can be incredibly frustrating, and without the right support and information it can feel like we're not being aspirational enough for our children.

Sensitive, attuned, confident and robust parenting is a cornerstone in assisting developmentally traumatized children to recover from the impact of their early years on their executive functions.

Shame

It is important to understand how shame is very different to guilt or embarrassment. To illustrate this, imagine the difference between making a mistake that you can ultimately laugh off or put right and a mistake you think reveals your true, terrible nature. Shame is an intensely painful feeling that you are fundamentally flawed. It is about who you *are*, not just what you have done. Shame can become the driving force behind how a person interacts with the world; for example, if they expect their inner awfulness to be revealed in interactions, they will seek to cover up their 'true' self or avoid situations in which this can happen.

Young children, before the age of around three, do not have the ability to understand other people's motivations, thoughts and mental states. This is important when we come to think about how our children experience and understand the abuse and neglect that they suffered in their early years.

Let's just take a moment to work through an example. Imagine you are hurt or abandoned by someone you love. Also imagine that you have no concept of their motivations. Therefore, all you have, to make sense of the world, is your own limited concept of your own drives, desires and feelings.

In this scenario what sense do you make of neglectful or abusive situations? Your only option is to absorb your experience as objective feedback about your interaction with others and the world. This leaves our children to process the abuse and neglect that they experience as the correct and inevitable response to their expression of need – believing it's something they deserve. If it seems to them that their need, something that is impulsive and compulsive, is deserving of such abuse and/or neglect, they can only develop feelings of shame for expressing something the world tells them they should not feel, something that is disgraceful and unacceptable. For example, if a child is hurt by their parent and there is no one communicating to them that a parent hurting a child is wrong, it is likely a child would understand it to be their fault.

Extreme and unavoidable shame is an inevitable consequence of early abuse and/or neglect. It is intolerable for all of us, and so we all work hard to escape that feeling. And an effective way of escaping an intolerable feeling is to defend against it. When children have been overdosed on shame, their subsequent reactions to even small amounts – such as typical reprimands – reawaken the hypersensitive reaction to earlier experiences of shame. This can take different behavioural forms, such as shouting, hitting out or masking your 'true' self.

Take a moment now to consider your reaction to something you have done that made you feel ashamed. Think about one of those cringe-worthy moments that we all tuck away in the recesses of our mind so we don't have to think about them. Then think about how you dealt with it.

Sometimes we might deny that we made the cringe-inducing faux pas; we might dismiss another person's hurt or offence as an overreaction; or we might pretend we don't care about the hurt person or their reaction to us.

When you consider these defensive strategies in relation to our developmentally traumatized children, I'm sure you will immediately think of many occasions on which your child has resorted to such strategies to avoid feeling bad.

To us it might seem like just a small amount of bad feeling that might help them to learn not to do something again. However, it's important that we understand that small amounts of shame immediately scratch at the barely healing wound of past, overwhelming and intolerable shame arising from their abuse and/ or neglect experiences.

The evaluative element of reward–punishment thinking and strategies require that children experience a little bit of shame – feeling a little bit bad about themselves to encourage them to avoid doing the thing that will result in shame. However, if a person has this hypersensitivity to shame, their defences will prevent them from being able to absorb and learn from the experience of shame. As a result, reward–punishment strategies are rarely effective with developmentally traumatized children.

Emotional regulation

Emotional or 'affect' regulation is crucial in understanding why we need an alternative to reward–punishment thinking. If you'd like more details, I'd recommend checking out my book, *Why Can't My Child Behave?*[34] However, it is useful to summarize emotional or 'affect' regulation and how it is crucial in understanding why we need an alternative to reward–punishment thinking.

In short, emotional regulation is a process that begins from birth. Babies require an adult to regulate their emotions for them in order that they can internalize the process for themselves. This intervention happens through constant adult regulation (via sensitivity, responsiveness expressed through soothing, rocking and calming). Ultimately this leads to babies and toddlers feeling confident (through experience) that emotions are manageable. In turn this enables children to develop the cognitive capacity to manage feelings.

To help bring this idea to life, think of what it is like being with a tiny baby. When very young babies have a problem, be it a hungry tummy or finding themselves rolled into an uncomfortable position, they have no way of managing their emotions about the problem. In order to deal with the problem and their own emotional response to it, they need to make sure someone else deals with it. Their problem becomes your problem. This gets less and less as babies develop the ability to regulate and manage emotion, for example, learning to sleep alone, waiting for food, etc. Until a baby's emotional reservoir is big enough to deal with any given issue, they need to use someone else's. The more they make use of someone else's emotional regulation skills, the more their own capacity for emotional regulation will grow.

Often, children who struggle with regulating their emotions will flip from 0 to 10 in a matter of moments. This can be over issues, which, from the outside, may seem trivial, like enforcing a bedtime or even stopping a child doing something risky that might hurt them. Anything with a 'no' involved can be prime territory for triggering extreme unregulated emotions in developmentally traumatized children.

The importance of emotional regulation when thinking about managing the behaviour of traumatized children is two-fold. First, when our children are faced with disapproval or the removal of some important or longed-for object, they may well find the emotional strain very difficult to regulate. Second, it may be that the behaviour we need to manage is the result of a struggle with regulating feelings. Expecting a child to be able to learn from reward–punishment strategies when they are emotionally **dysregulated** (that is, when emotions seem disproportionately heightened and uncontrollable) makes about as much sense as punishing anxiety or sadness. That's not to say that dysregulated feelings don't need managing; they very much do. The need is much greater, in fact, than the need for managing tricky behaviour. However, we simply cannot regulate feelings by punishing them. It doesn't work.

The best strategy is to make every effort we can to make those feelings smaller, not bigger. When we bring in all the relational and emotional strain of reward–punishment thinking, it's often the latter that happens. We can actually make children's behaviour worse by increasing their emotional dysregulation.

When we collect together the neurological and other scientific evidence and, to be honest, even more powerfully for me, the repeated stories of families coping with trauma, we come to the resounding conclusion that reward–punishment thinking simply isn't the most effective way. It doesn't stop the most common challenging behaviours our children present us with, it doesn't build happier, more connected families, and it doesn't improve the emotional and mental wellbeing of children traumatized by abuse and/or neglect.

So why is reward–punishment thinking still the logic that we most commonly use in our parenting? We know about how it came to be, via Skinner's work in the last century; we also know about the neurological evidence that should move us away from reward–punishment thinking. To understand why the old approach still carries such power, we also need to look beyond a logical analysis of the available evidence.

One of the most compelling explanations about why we keep repeatedly using strategies without any evidence of success is located in new evidence about the way in which humans make decisions, which is not as logical or as rational as we tell ourselves it is.

How we really make decisions

Recent psychological discovery has taught us some incredible things about how we make decisions.[35] Children make 'decisions' about their behaviour in a similarly automatic and intuitive way as adults make their decisions about parenting.

The vast majority of our decisions are made by the automatic, emotional 'system one' in our brains, not the more rational, slow, deliberate and comparatively scarcely used 'system two' that we tend to think of as 'us', our moral core, our character. We'll refer to 'system one' as our 'Hare' system – impulsive, fast and error-prone – and to 'system two' as our 'Tortoise' system – slow, deliberate and analytical.

Tortoise and Hare decision-making systems

The evidence of these two competing systems surrounds us. Who of us, when making an important decision – what house to live in, which political party to vote for, who to live with – can truly and honestly justify their decision as based only on facts and rational analysis?

We make these, and most other decisions, with our gut. However, when asked to justify our decisions, we rarely, if ever, feel able to refer to our emotional, irrational, Hare system drives. We either deny the influence of this system or we don't even acknowledge it ourselves – we're supposed to be better than to allow such 'silly' impulses to control our decision-making. But it is universal and so self-defeating to not acknowledge it. It's ridiculous and dangerous for societies as a whole to fail to talk about the reality on which the majority of our decisions depend. At its worst it results in a bamboozling double-think, whereby we try to justify our Hare system decisions, such as buying new clothes we can't afford, by conjuring up Tortoise system rationalizations; for example, 'none of my old ones are suitable'. This only serves to defend our decisions and not to enable understanding, acceptance or scrutiny of what is really driving our behaviour.

We are learning more and more about how fixed and unchangeable the Hare system is, yet parenting books tend to focus on telling us that it's the impulsive things that need to change by over-ruling our Hare system with our Tortoise system. When we're under stress, this is incredibly difficult, if not impossible. The truth of the matter is that, day to day, we don't even really accept the existence of our Hare system decision-making. We tell ourselves and our children that we must not use this 35-million-year-old, evolutionarily hard-wired, cast-in-stone system (our predominant way of navigating our lives) by sheer force of will. It's as though discipline is our only route to change. Generally, in our culture, failure to exercise discipline (over our own impulses and those of our children) is viewed with disdain and condemnation; for example, unhealthy eating, illicit drug use, anti-social behaviour.

I was particularly struck by the power of this phenomenon when watching the documentary film *Amy* about the life and death of Amy Winehouse. The film recalls that Amy was told that she would die unless she stopped drinking. She is desperate not to die; her rational system decided not to drink alcohol but was overridden by her impulsive system. Her behaviour was compulsive; she couldn't stop it, no matter how much she wanted to. It certainly wasn't because the consequences weren't severe enough or because Amy didn't understand the 'rules'. It was more that the link between cause and effect wasn't powerful enough and/or that the fear of the consequences didn't do anything to diminish the impulsive desirability of drinking more alcohol.

Given the impaired executive functions of those of us who have experienced developmental trauma, it stands to reason that fostered and adopted children will often have an even more dominant Hare system than those who have not experienced such trauma.

Reward–punishment thinking leads us to believe that the Tortoise systems of developmentally traumatized children can be pumped up enough by practice and discipline to dominate their Hare systems, despite repeated committed efforts and devastating failures. Using this logic, we stop looking at the evidence about what has or hasn't worked and keep doing what we've always done because that's what our biased Hare system tells us to. Think, for example, of when we frustratedly raise our voices and tell a child to get back into bed and go to sleep when we can see that they are full of energy.

One of the core principles of Empathic Behaviour Management (EBM), or what we will go on to call 'superparenting', is the understanding and acceptance not only of our children's automatic decision-making but also of our own. We accept that changing our automatic, impulsive reactions is a very hit and miss business, that perhaps it is impossible. Acceptance of our underlying characters, defaults and emotions is the key to adapting our surroundings (including our behaviours and those of our children) to make living with those Hare system decisions more harmonious, more connected and more satisfying.

We have fully considered the parenting approaches that most of us default to, the unique needs of traumatized children and the real way in which we make our parenting decisions. It is now time to turn to an alternative, a way in which we can be compassionate to our own needs and those of our child in a targeted, realistic and effective way.

What is superparenting?

Superparenting is most certainly *not* perfect parenting. It is simply a way of summarizing the 'extra' that it takes to be a therapeutic parent and just how hard it can be. Superparents embark on a journey that requires extra tenacity, patience, understanding, commitment, energy and, most crucially, extra analysis and scrutiny of themselves as a tool to understand and support their children. It is as much the willingness to do that as it is the techniques I can offer that makes them 'super'. The willingness to make those sacrifices and dig so deep is indeed a superpower, borne of a refusal to give up, and the deepest, truest kind of love, even when love may be hard to feel.

What is Empathic Behaviour Management (EBM)?

The following chapters which, in honour of the superhuman effort that parents and carers of traumatized children put in, we will call 'superpowers', will guide you through the detail of what EBM is and how it helps us to maintain our 'superparenting' approach. I will also guide you through what it isn't, and how it is similar and different to traditional reward–punishment parenting.

Fundamentally, EBM is a way of parenting therapeutically whilst being mindful of managing behaviour. It is a therapeutic parenting method that incorporates the particular psychological, emotional and neurological needs of children traumatized by abuse and/or neglect. It doesn't dodge or skirt around some of the most challenging behaviours we face, and it provides a way of tackling such behaviours compassionately and assertively in the most effective way we have.

EBM is compatible with several therapeutic parenting approaches and most notably some models of therapeutic intervention, such as **Dyadic Developmental Psychotherapy (DDP)**, which is a therapy based on the potential of healthy, therapeutic parenting relationships to heal relational trauma[36, 37] and, to a certain extent, **Non-Violent Resistance (NVR)**, a form of systemic family therapy, which has been developed for aggressive, violent, controlling and self-destructive behaviour in young people.[38]

Traditional reward–punishment parenting invites us into a trap when it comes to dealing with the behaviour of children traumatized by abuse and/or neglect. Many parents and carers assume – in fact they are encouraged to believe – that a difficult behaviour must be directly trained out of a child with rewards and punishments. Also, that a necessary by-product of this might well be the need for confrontation, and that without it those behaviours will continue and possibly even escalate. Many parents feel that they are failing in their parenting responsibility if they do not take the tough way and risk falling out with their child in order to discipline them out of behaving a certain way.

EBM encourages us to understand that conflict and disconnection in parenting is a sure-fire indication that it isn't working and that we are engaging via coercion and force rather than through connection and strength. That's not to say that parents don't still have to make unpopular decisions; they certainly do. In EBM we emphasize reconnection (not necessarily changing your unpopular viewpoint) as the priority.

The following chapters will also refer to the need for assertive parenting and being able to calm the rough seas of upsetting our children when we need to take a parenting decision that they don't want us to take. A common confusion, when exploring empathic, connected parenting, is to assume that it requires parents to be laissez-faire and unassertive in their dealings with their children. EBM is not 'permissive'; it simply encourages us to think more about how our parenting makes our children (and us) feel, and parent accordingly.

Approaches and techniques

In order to understand the difference that EBM brings, we have to think about 'approaches'; that is, the theory and logic that underpins different ways of parenting, and the 'techniques', the day-to-day strategies and habits that we use in response to our children's behaviour.

There is a radical difference between reward–punishment and EBM approaches. Sometimes, however, the different approaches lead us to use techniques that are identical; for example, increasing structure and routine for a chaotic disorganized child. On some occasions the techniques that extend from the different approaches are only subtly different but different all the same; for example, the difference between praise and celebrating success when faced with a 14-year-old boy who has cleaned his teeth for the first time in a week. On other occasions the traditional reward–punishment and EBM approaches to parenting lead us to use extremely different techniques, and sometimes these are completely contradictory. For example, in the face of a 6-year-old shouting and swearing at her brother, a traditional reward–punishment approach may lead us to use time out. This necessitates space between us and our child, and uses our absence as a consequence for their behaviour. This leads us to ignore our child and convey disapproval, in the belief that this will deter the child from doing such a thing again in the future. An EBM approach would lead us to do the exact opposite and bring the child closer to us to use physical proximity and increased warmth and connection to regulate their emotions and thereby stop the problematic behaviour.

No matter whether the difference in the technique is huge and obvious or subtle and nuanced, the difference between the approach, the guiding principles of these parenting techniques, is enormous. An EBM approach means we can convey difference in our body language and facial expressions as well as in our words and behaviour. These are the magical ingredients that enable us to produce astoundingly different results in children's behaviour, emotions and their connections with us and with the rest of the world.

The importance of language

It might seem that differentiating between approaches, when the techniques are sometimes similar, is pedantic. If the techniques are the same or similar, then 'Why make such a big fuss? Let's just adapt what we do a bit'. The problem is that the reward–punishment groove is so well worn in parenting that when trying to depart from it, the slightest wobble causes us to fall straight back in. We need a mind shift, a fresh, exciting, exhilaratingly hopeful way of thinking. As a result, a whole new logic and language is required. This can create distance from that cavernous groove, with its slippery edges and its murky, unsatisfying bottom.

I propose that we take a good, hard look at what 'boundaries', 'consequences', 'consistency', 'praise', etc. really and practically mean for us and our developmentally traumatized children. Let's take a step back and look at our children's needs, including their behaviour management needs, through the lens of their emotional and psychological development. Let's reclaim 'parenting' and think more about what makes children function well and happily, rather than over-simplifying parenting as only ensuring children are well-behaved. We will refocus on language such as 'safety', 'security', 'containment', 'connection' and 'support'.

In the following chapters I will continue to emphasize this point, so that we can correct the mistaken (but commonly held) notion that prioritizing children's emotional worlds and psychological health means being permissive, laissez-faire or even lazy in our parenting.

When parents and carers first come to me and we discuss leaving behind reward–punishment strategies and taking up empathic habits, they will sometimes say things like 'I'm just not going to let them…shout at me/throw their food/smash things'. If these are some of the worries you have, then please, let me reassure you: using empathic strategies does not necessarily mean accepting these things and certainly not those things that particularly press your buttons and cause more distance in your relationship with your child.

When faced with the assertion from parents and carers that 'He's got to learn', I agree wholeheartedly! And I also empathize deeply with the frustration implied. The problem in focusing on making children learn comes from the fact that we, as a culture, are encouraged to believe that reward–punishment strategies are the only active way to help children learn and to create change in our family lives. Empathic, relationship-focused alternatives are not only more effective for children traumatized by abuse and neglect, but they work, not in spite of their gentleness, but because of it. It is only possible to get through to a frightened, distanced child via consent and connection; attempts to force or coerce our way in will only build stronger walls of defence.

Dropping those reward–punishment strategies, with all of their seductive immediacy and satisfying feelings of justice, does not mean losing hope of change; it means adjustment to achieving that change differently.

The EBM approach is a hugely practical one. The majority of parents and carers of traumatized children have dedicatedly and tirelessly tried all of those traditional reward–punishment strategies that they are told to or that worked so successfully with their birth children. Many have lost heart or are bogged down in frustrated annoyance because the techniques that they have worked so hard on have had little effect on their traumatized child. It is likely that you have found your way to this book because you've already tried all of the well-worn, recommended, reward–punishment strategies. EBM is certainly no magic wand, but it can undercut much of this frustrated expectation, build better relationships and help your child to heal.

To adjust to empathic, attachment-driven habits, we need to change our mindsets a little. It can be easier to imagine this shift by comparing the urge to continue to apply a reward–punishment approach (even when we see it is not solving the problem) as similar to treating a toothache by constantly combating the pain with analgesics rather than trying to treat the underlying infection by taking antibiotics.

Each chapter will discuss and explore a 'parenting power', first through a reward–punishment lens and then through an EBM lens. By the end of the book, you should have a clear, practical understanding of each 'superpower' and how they will help you to parent your developmentally traumatized child (and maximize their healing) from an empathic, attachment-based point of view, whilst also being clear about the difficult reward–punishment pitfalls that we can all be pulled towards.

It is also useful to prepare ourselves to view parenting as a set of habits rather than necessarily instant strategies. Rarely, with developmentally traumatized children, does anything work immediately. Getting used to the language of 'parenting habits' helps us to think longer term when expecting to see the fruits of our considerable labour. We don't expect to keep healthy teeth by brushing them studiously for a single week; we integrate it into our routines and expect to have to do it every day. Helping our children grow past their trauma requires similarly permanent and persistent habits.

Traditional parenting approaches and their therapeutic alternatives

Traditional parenting approach	Therapeutic parenting (EBM) alternative
Parental self-discipline	Parental self-acceptance
Boundaries	Safe containment
Praise	Celebration or sharing joy
Reassurance	Sharing difficult feelings
Consistency	Responsivity
Being 'in control of'	Being 'in control for'
Force	Strength
Evaluation	Exploring 'why?'
Behavioural change	Emotional acceptance
'Weaning off' dependency	'Filling up' or accepting dependency needs
Rewards	Building motivation and hope
Structure and routine: behavioural containment	Structure and routine: safety and emotional containment

PARENTAL SELF-ACCEPTANCE

Introduction

One of the cornerstones of traditional parenting philosophies is that, in times of trouble, it is useful for parents to learn new approaches and strategies, and then it is up to parents to apply that knowledge with their children. Sounds straightforward and pretty good common sense, right? Let's explore.

In order to consider this thoroughly, let's think about having the parallel expectation of children. In the book's Introduction we concluded that most of the time it is an illusion to expect developmentally traumatized children to be able to simply act on what we have taught, coached and disciplined into them. Their Hare system is just too dominant. We obviously expect more of ourselves as adults, but there are a few very good reasons why we might need to cut ourselves a bit more slack.

The Tortoise and the Hare

Let's take the time to remind ourselves about these two very different but complementary decision-making systems and how they influence parenting. Understanding these systems is crucial in helping us to prioritize self-acceptance over self-discipline in children and parents alike.

The Tortoise

The Tortoise represents slow-thinking decision-making and parenting the way we ideally want to.

Meet the Tortoise. She's a calm and thoughtful type. She takes her time and comes up with the most considered, reliable parenting plans. She's rational and considered and would *never* overreact, shout at her child or threaten to take away the TV for a 'a whole year!' (even when TV time is the only way she gets a break) or threaten to ground a child until they're 30… The Tortoise would be far more likely to follow through on the sensible parenting plans she had made in the cold light of day.

Our Tortoise decision-making comprises the collection of thoughts about our ideal way of parenting, the decisions we make actively and with forethought. Often, we make promises to ourselves and perhaps to our partners about the kind of parent we want to be. For example, 'I won't hit my kids', 'I want our kids to get into a routine', 'I really want to listen to my child'. These parenting plans are often based on our own experiences of being parented. They can also come from looking at what friends and family do, ways of parenting we see in the popular media, TV, etc.

Most sources of parenting advice are fantastic at impacting on this type of decision-making. However, they can become a significant part of the self-discipline narrative – if you try hard enough, you will crack any problems you may have with your child's behaviour. When that inevitably fails, it can all too often lead to disillusionment, frustration and shame, particularly for parents under stress. Some of you will have been there; you've found the book or the approach that fits so completely with how you want to parent that you become evangelical: 'I have found the answer!' You read, you study, you plan, you talk to friends about your epiphany. You may well have some significant success. However, when the acute stress of looking after a traumatized child hits, your fabulous intentions go out of the window and you feel that you've failed (or that your child has failed).

The (maybe meagre) salvation that I can offer from the impending despair is simply to know that it was inevitable; we cannot maintain such aspirational ideals under such extreme stress. *It's…not…possible.* So many parents, after repeated experience of this, will feel despair, like they're inadequate, overwhelmed and just not good enough. But here's a radically liberating idea: maybe failing sometimes is actually okay. Maybe the answer is in finding more acceptance for our imperfect selves.

We need to correct this belief that once the decision is made to parent in this way that the psychological work is done, that you will (or should be able to) be consistent in your approach – under stress it is unlikely to be that straightforward. The 'the two steps forward, one step back' metaphor might be a more realistic expectation. The decisions you have proactively made about your parenting are still there even when you have parented in a way you really didn't want to. The reward–punishment narrative about consistency can mean that we don't forgive ourselves very readily. Your task after these events is to acknowledge what has happened and accept the extraordinary circumstances that have got you there. Be kind to yourself and feel sorry that you have to experience such challenges. Then acknowledge and examine what has got you to that tough place and use your understanding to move back to where you want to be and carry on carrying on until the next time.

The decisions we make about parenting are the standards to which we aspire, the expectations that we hold ourselves to. When we are trying to exercise self-discipline (more than self-acceptance) in times of extraordinary pressure, we judge ourselves by these aspirational standards and beat ourselves up with them.

When we are exercising self-acceptance, we still aspire to our parenting goals; after all, they are crucial, they are how we want to raise our children. The difference between this approach and traditional self-discipline is that after we stray from our parenting goals, under pressure, we take a different route. We don't silently criticize ourselves. We acknowledge and nurture our own inevitable frailty. We actively notice, with wonder and curiosity, how our external and internal worlds impact on our ability to achieve our parenting goals.

The Hare

The Hare represents fast-thinking decision-making, parenting the way that feels right in the moment.

Allow me to introduce you to the Hare. She's an energetic sort who gets things done. She's busy all day, every day, and can get carried away. With everything she has to do, she can make the odd bad decision. She is most definitely the one who might overreact and threaten to ban all screen time for a year.

Often parents and carers are expecting high levels of self-discipline from themselves. When dealing with tricky, traumatized children, it is very easy to become desperately disappointed and ashamed that they have found themselves veering away from their carefully thought-out (or intuitively known) parenting goals. Most parents are hopeful, when they seek help, that their professional can help them to override their Hare system. They want a way to replace their Hare impulses with their Tortoise parenting, that is, the parenting they do when they are fully recharged and firing on all cylinders. It is tragic and fascinating in equal measure that we honestly hold this expectation that we should be immune from the impacts of trauma in our parent–child relationships when we 'know' how impactful they are.

Although there are a few grounding techniques (see below) that can help us to deploy our Tortoise system rather than our Hare system, our most powerful tool is self-acceptance and mindfulness. So, let's dive headfirst into self-acceptance; let's name and acknowledge what happens when we lose the ability to execute our parenting goals as we would like to. In doing so we therefore empower ourselves to examine how disconnections happen and how to get the relationships with our children back to where we want them to be.

In short, even the best functioning brains in the most emotionally settled of states do not make most decisions in a rational way. We make most of our decisions quickly and intuitively, using our fast-thinking Hare decision-making process. Under stress our decision-making processes are challenged even further by our impaired executive function and emotional dysregulation. This applies to all of us, and as much as we would like to think we are in control of what we do, neurology tells us otherwise. The stress of looking after a traumatized child who is defending against shame and suffering from the effects of toxic stress creates one of the most challenging environments for rational thinking there is. Yet, we put such mystifyingly high expectations on ourselves and expect parenting *knowledge* to smoothly transfer into parenting *practice*, even in these toughest of scenarios.

We cannot, simply cannot, parent in the way we want to all of the time. We all know this, yet we are pretty terrible at accepting ourselves when we deviate from 'the plan'. How does it feel when this happens? What things do parents tell themselves when they fail in their stressed-out Hare states? Many parents and carers start out feeling disappointed, frustrated and annoyed, but often move to feeling despairing, angry and ashamed. They tell themselves they've failed, that they're not good enough, sometimes, heartbreakingly, that this is proof that they were never supposed to be parents. They can get as far down this torturous way of thinking as to tell themselves that their situation is hopeless. And all of this self-persecution is down to the flawed expectation that parenting is as simple as having enough self-discipline to override our impulsive Hare decision-making system and put into practice the strategies that we know we 'should'.

The destructive potential of 'shoulds'

Of all the families I've worked with, there isn't a single one that hasn't tortured themselves with 'shoulds' about themselves or their children: 'I know I *should* have stopped him', 'She *should* be able to do this!' or 'I know I *should*n't have done it'. The prevalence of 'shoulds' is a vivid example of how instinctive it is to expect discipline in ourselves and in others, and how challenging it is to accept ourselves and our impulsive Hare system.

Rather than 'shoulds' it would be useful to try and take a more accepting, mindful approach – first, in relation to our own behaviour. For example, when you haven't parented the way you want to, you could try an internal monologue, something like 'Ooh, that's interesting. I shouted at her. I had definitely decided I really didn't want to do that. I wonder how I got there. I'm going to try and remember this and try to notice when it happens again and when it doesn't!' Okay, you might still beat yourself up a bit first, but allowing yourself some space from the self-flagellation might just take you somewhere more positive.

Taking this more nurturing approach towards ourselves opens our thinking, encourages us to be curious and open-minded and allows us to think creatively. It engages us in really understanding what is going on to make us behave in a way we definitely ('really, absolutely definitely, *definitely* this time') weren't going to.

Drowning ourselves in 'shoulds', on the other hand, stops us from wondering and encourages us to continue banging on the same unsatisfying door. This can easily spiral into disappointment, feelings of inadequacy, and disconnection between parent and child.

Post-hoc rationalizations: when shame leads to false justification

The other issue we parents and carers encounter when trying to exercise self-discipline rather than self-acceptance is feeling the need to justify ourselves when we act on anything but fully thought-through, rational parenting intentions. When parenting is at its toughest, our impulsive Hare system decision-making kicks in, often resulting in shouting, impatience or even physical punishment. At these times the belief that parents should be disciplined enough to override their Hare system often results in shame and makes us look for a way out of that shame. A very useful way out of shame is to tell ourselves that we meant to behave the way we did and that it's part of an intended approach: 'Well, how will she learn if she doesn't know she's done something wrong?', 'There have to be consequences for that, I'm not going to put up with it', 'I'm not doing him any favours if I let him get away with it'.

It's worth noting that post-hoc rationalizations (gut reactions first, think up the reasons later) come up an enormous amount for developmentally traumatized children too, not just for their parents and carers, but we will cover that later in the book.

To help us in our goal towards self-acceptance, it is useful to explore why our Hare systems can lead us down a parenting path that we never wanted to travel down. This knowledge can give us something with which to soothe the anxiously critical voices in our heads when telling us that we have failed in our self-discipline.

What *is it* that makes our Hare system unhelpful and not therapeutic?

Why is it, when we're making quick, impulsive parenting decisions under stress, that they are more likely than not to be unhelpful ones?

First, we need to accept that in those end-of-our-tether moments, we do impulsively *want* to shout, hit, criticize and dismiss our children. We do indeed feel satisfaction from this. When the pressure cooker has filled to this extent, it is cathartic to vent the frustrated, furious steam. Acceptance of this fact helps us to appreciate our needs and prevent building shame and thus defensive post-hoc rationalizations. As detailed in the book's Introduction, however, this approach generally leads nowhere good for either ourselves or for our children.

Punitive parenting resulting from frustration or anger

Exhaustion, unachievable expectations and the frustration of caring for a child who may not know how to 'do' relationships makes parenting traumatized children tough. It also means that our Hare system is likely to be driven by the under-siege, primitive areas of our brain, which are specialized to help us in times of threat. When we are under threat, we default to our survival instincts. When stress levels are high and fuses are short, it is a default response to react in anger and with a passionate drive for justice. It is incredibly difficult, no matter who you are, to access empathy and reasonable thought when you are under such high levels of pressure.

The default actions, or rather reactions, that come easily to our grasp at these times are those that meet our emotional needs. It is instinctive to want to see the person who has caused our extreme distress in a similar amount of distress and discomfort. This is, in essence, the feeling of justice.

In this way it is very easy to end up using punitive strategies when we are under pressure with our traumatized children. When these things happen, it is very important that we do not judge or blame ourselves. The danger is not that these things will happen; the real jeopardy is that we feel such shame about our reaction that we escape the shame by not acknowledging it. When this happens, we allow ourselves to absorb the strategy into our parenting tool box and then justify it after the event (a post-hoc rationalization).

Reactive parenting resulting from burnout or blocked care

Burnout and **blocked care** are, sadly for all concerned, tremendously common amongst adults looking after developmentally traumatized children.

> Blocked care describes how stress can suppress a well-meaning parent's capacity to sustain loving feelings and empathy towards his or her child.[39]

Blocked care is a neurological process whereby repeated unsatisfactory, non-reciprocal and/or aversive parenting experiences lead parents to shut down their attunement in order to avoid the relational pain caused by emotional connection; in short, when a parent–child relationship becomes so painful and unsatisfying that a parent becomes emotionally detached to protect themselves.

In this state the main focus often turns to reactive parenting and fast, short-term change, such as getting a child to pick up the thrown food off the floor rather than understanding the rage that caused the food to be thrown. Challenging behaviour can feel so much more challenging in this state. In response, our impulsive Hare system is heightened, and our rational Tortoise system is impaired. We tend to be less empathic, not only towards our children, but also towards ourselves. As a result, we can so easily spiral (via post-hoc rationalizations and shame) into parenting that is a million miles away from where we want to be. Parents in blocked care also often experience low mood, depression, despair and/or rage.

Reactive parenting as a result of relationship replication (aka transference and countertransference)

Put simply, transference is when a child (in this case) behaves with you in accordance with how they expect you to be (that is, how they have learned primary carers will be). Countertransference means you (in this case) ending up behaving in the way your children expect you to, based on their past experience.

How do children's expectations of adults' behaviour develop? Through their experience of adults' behaviour. In the case of developmentally traumatized children, it is their early, traumatizing experience that shapes their expectations.

How our expectations make us behave in relationships

All of us have expectations of the world and relationships that come from our early experience.

If, in our formative weeks and months, we are exposed to gentle, kind and sensitive treatment from those we rely on, we will internalize that as an unconscious expectation of the people we interact with in the world.

If, however, we have an early experience of our expressions of need being met with fury, shouting, roughness or even violence, we will carry *these* expectations of relationships into later life. No matter what our experience of early life is, the expectations that result become hard-wired into our neurological make-up.

These relationship expectations then tell us what the most appropriate ways to behave in any given relationship are.

So how do we behave in relationships when we expect kindness and sensitivity? We begin with openness and trust and a willingness to engage with other people. In mid-childhood, for example, this may look like smiles, eye contact, chattiness and an ability to trust that adult instruction is given to keep you safe.

Conversely, how do we behave in relationships when we expect anger, hostility or rejection? We approach such relationships with a sense of mistrust, fear and reservation.

How our experience-based behaviour triggers others to behave towards us

To continue with the two examples above, let's think about what our reactions would be to the two scenarios above.

How does this mid-childhood behaviour encourage others to relate to these people?

First, the child is engaging, trusting and communicative. In general, that child will make us feel engaged, effective and satisfied with the relationship. We behave in ways that stem from these feelings; we are calm, we listen, and we engage positively with this child. Therefore, we enact the positive roles that are expected, intuitively, of us.

Now the child who mistrusts us and is aloof with us – how does this child's approach to relationships invite us to interact? Someone who is, from the off, incredibly challenging to engage with can lead to people feeling put off from trying to build a relationship with them. Consequently, our Hare system leads us to be aloof, disengaged and superficial in our engagement with this child. Therefore aloof, mistrustful behaviour leads us to be worthy of the expectation that it implies.

Relationships often become a kind of self-fulfilling prophecy; the way we behave towards another person (based on our relational expectations) invites them to behave in the way we expect of them.

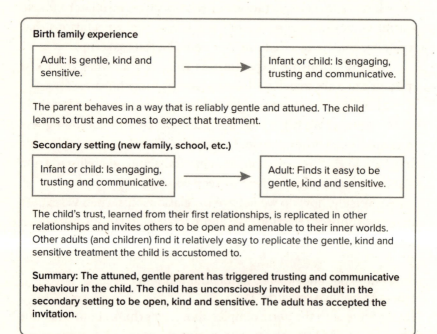

Birth family experience

Adult: Is gentle, kind and sensitive. → Infant or child: Is engaging, trusting and communicative.

The parent behaves in a way that is reliably gentle and attuned. The child learns to trust and comes to expect that treatment.

Secondary setting (new family, school, etc.)

Infant or child: Is engaging, trusting and communicative. → Adult: Finds it easy to be gentle, kind and sensitive.

The child's trust, learned from their first relationships, is replicated in other relationships and invites others to be open and amenable to their inner worlds. Other adults (and children) find it relatively easy to replicate the gentle, kind and sensitive treatment the child is accustomed to.

Summary: The attuned, gentle parent has triggered trusting and communicative behaviour in the child. The child has unconsciously invited the adult in the secondary setting to be open, kind and sensitive. The adult has accepted the invitation.

Relationship replication: happy and healthy (enough) family

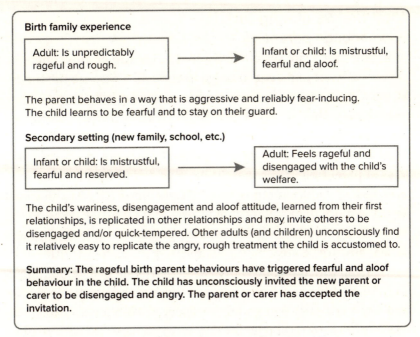

Birth family experience

| Adult: Is unpredictably rageful and rough. | → | Infant or child: Is mistrustful, fearful and aloof. |

The parent behaves in a way that is aggressive and reliably fear-inducing. The child learns to be fearful and to stay on their guard.

Secondary setting (new family, school, etc.)

| Infant or child: Is mistrustful, fearful and reserved. | → | Adult: Feels rageful and disengaged with the child's welfare. |

The child's wariness, disengagement and aloof attitude, learned from their first relationships, is replicated in other relationships and may invite others to be disengaged and/or quick-tempered. Other adults (and children) unconsciously find it relatively easy to replicate the angry, rough treatment the child is accustomed to.

Summary: The rageful birth parent behaviours have triggered fearful and aloof behaviour in the child. The child has unconsciously invited the new parent or carer to be disengaged and angry. The parent or carer has accepted the invitation.

Relationship replication: early trauma

Acting on blocked care or relationship replication

Acting on blocked care	You find yourself acting in ways you don't recognize
	You feel a loss of joy in your relationship with your child despite being able to physically look after them
	You have become the type of parent that you don't want to be
	Things that your child does that other people think are okay make you snap, criticize or shout
	You feel numb to, or annoyed by, your child's emotions and expressions of need
	It is difficult to think through your parenting approach
	You feel demotivated from trying to understand what is going on in your child's head
Acting on relationship replication	You seem to be inadvertently making your child feel the way they did in their abusive past
	You find yourself acting in ways you don't recognize
	You have become the type of parent that you don't want to be
	Your child's behaviour seems to 'invite' you to behave in a way you wouldn't ordinarily

What are we aiming for?
Good-enough parenting

Sometimes the Hare system decision-making can be close enough to how we want to parent to be 'good enough'. These are the times we manage to hold on to some semblance of empathy. They are the tough times when we somehow avoid creating (further) distance from our child.

At other times our Hare systems lead us to 'not good-enough' ways of parenting. It's at these times that self-acceptance enables us to reflect and then repair the relationships with our children. Repair is more than simply apologizing. It is an active decision to put aside annoyance (when possible), boundaries and discipline; in fact, any urge to teach. It is an assertive move to prioritize our relationship with our child above all else, a true act of unconditional love. An attitude of self-discipline at these times is more likely to lead us to self-criticism and defensiveness. Nobody ever made a relationship better again whilst they were preoccupied with shame and defensiveness.

Balancing your needs with the needs of your child

Let's lay this on the table – parenting traumatized children changes you. It changes you in the moment (your impulsive Hare system) and, without a lot of reflection and support, it is almost certain to change your overarching goals and perspective on parenting (your rational Tortoise system).

So much of the parenting advice for parents and carers of traumatized children does not take into account the changes that happen to adults who care for traumatized children. The focus of that, sometimes fantastic, advice is on the way parents can do things differently. This is fabulous...if it works. In reality, it is necessary to acknowledge parents' own triggers (their own frailties, parenting histories and expectations) and needs rather than just giving advice as though parents can just ignore or override their internal challenges.

We now understand the extraordinary stress of looking after our children, the impact of stress on our pre-frontal cortex (which controls our executive function) and the dominance of the Hare system. Ignoring these things and focusing on parenting without focusing on parents sets people up to fail. Just as setting out our behavioural expectations of traumatized children rarely works (and, in fact, just raises shame), expecting the same from highly stressed adults is just as doomed to fail.

There are a few techniques that can work powerfully for parents in the moment to help them to ground themselves (see below). However, the most useful technique for managing those difficult in-the-moment feelings is acceptance – acceptance of children via acceptance of ourselves. One way of achieving acceptance like this is to use mindfulness (see Parenting Superpower #6).

We must therefore get comfortable with the idea that parenting traumatized children requires parents to be clear and assertive with themselves about the necessity of balancing their child's needs with their own. Without that balance, blocked care and burnout are far more likely and sadly, in reality, all too common.

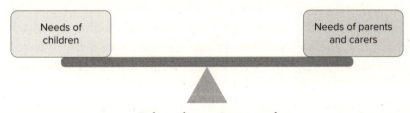

Balanced attention to need

It is very easy to move either side of this balance. To be too focused on parents' or children's needs is to the detriment of the other and, most importantly, to the detriment of the relationship that holds you together.

One of the traps that parents and carers often fall into is routine self-sacrifice because *that's what adults 'should' do* for children, especially vulnerable children. This can mean walking on eggshells so as not to upset a child or young person, not imposing rules through fear of a child or young person's response, giving more time and attention than you feel able to sustain – generally, not looking after your own needs. This works when stress is short term and the sacrifice pays off. It simply isn't a sustainable strategy when you're parenting a developmentally traumatized child. You *are* the tool your child so desperately needs to help them develop positivity and trust in relationships. Sustaining yourself and therefore your ability to parent *must* be your top priority. Without it no one will do well.

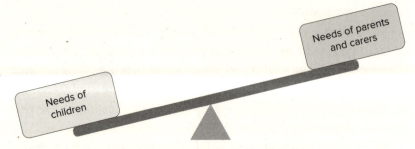

Weightier attention to children's needs

It is equally common to move to the other side of that balance (often due to desperate self-preservation). This is when care and empathy diminish because the needs of children appear reduced through exhausted and battle-weary eyes. In these circumstances parents inevitably perceive their needs as being higher than their children's. The parent–child dynamic then becomes a disconnected one and can, simply through pain, heartache and complete and utter exhaustion, descend (through self-preservation) into punitive, cold and/or hostile interactions. Heartbreakingly, this often happens when parents and carers start from a position of self-sacrifice and then become entirely overwhelmed by it.

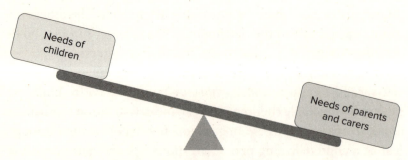

Weightier attention to parents' needs

Commonly, when parents tip over to the punitive side of the balance, they feel (often very justifiably) bullied or victimized. They may feel that their child is deliberately and selfishly choosing to take more from them than they can bear: 'Why can't they just stop?! Can't they see this is too hard for everyone?!' This can lead to the temptation to pass off a child's overwhelming level of need as 'just' 'naughtiness', 'wilfulness' or something pathological: 'There's something wrong with her!'

In this position, which we can all find ourselves slipping into and out of, it is natural and understandable to be drawn to reward–punishment thinking, but it isn't often helpful in the long term. It can also be the case that all we want to hear is how terrible or impossible to care for the child is. It is incredibly difficult at these times to connect with empathy and feel a child's genuinely high level of need. Doing so would mean reconnecting with that need and the potentially overwhelming emotions and demands that this entails. This dynamic all too commonly becomes literally unbearable, and leads to adoption disruption or placements breaking down.

It is crucial therefore to try and avoid the seesaw tipping too far in either direction. As in all things, balance and moderation is maddeningly necessary when it comes to whose needs should take priority.

When trying to find this balance, we are challenged with, very consciously, differentiating what is for your benefit and what is for your child's. It can be very tempting, for example, to insist on an early bedtime because your child is 'tired', when the real motivation is your need for half an hour of 'me time' to keep yourself together. It is difficult to be honest about asserting our need for these things because we are taught to believe that self-discipline and sacrifice are the only 'good' parenting strategies. Guilt and shame can predominate when we prioritize our own needs. Hopefully it is starting to become clear that this logic simply doesn't make sense if we want to sustain the relationships that our children so desperately need.

To demonstrate exactly how the traditional and EBM approaches and techniques may be similar or different, we will explore what may be typical responses to real-life scenarios. This will help us to explore what EBM is all about (and what it isn't). As well as looking at what each of the approaches would have us aspire to, we will also explore a more real-life example of how our exhausted Hare might react.

✸ YOLANDA

Yolanda is an adoptive mum. She's exhausted. She has two children, one of whom wants attention from her, for what feels like 24 hours a day, 7 days a week, asking her seemingly continuous questions and needing to chat constantly. He struggles to entertain himself for more than a few seconds at a time. Her other son struggles to follow any instruction from his mum. Asking him to do anything, from putting his clothes in the wash basket to sitting down to eat his tea, ends in conflict and often makes Yolanda feel like she has a choice between escalating things into screaming tantrums or giving up on even having basic requests followed.

Yolanda has listened to her family and taken advice from a couple of professionals who work with her. She's tried so incredibly hard, hour after hour, day after day, and year after year. She loves her children so much and she feels like she's failed them. Yolanda thinks she's no good at being a parent. She has shouted at her children and been rougher with them than she would have liked. She feels like she's rejected them when all they have wanted is a cuddle. She feels guilty and 'not good enough' all the time.

Reality: the exhausted Hare	Traditional: self-discipline	Therapeutic: self-acceptance
✗	✗	✓
(Unpredictable)	(Not trauma-informed)	(Trauma-informed)

Comparison of approaches

Reality: the exhausted Hare
Approach

The exhausted Hare 'approach' is the way parenting often gets done, particularly by parents and carers trying their hardest to look after challenging, developmentally traumatized children. This is not what any of us would necessarily consider the ideal way of doing things, but, given the stresses and strains of this kind of 'superparenting', it's real and might well be 'good enough'.

The exhausted Hare can only wryly be called an approach, as it's not really as organized as the word 'approach' suggests. However, the overarching parenting drive of the exhausted Hare is to get their house running in as harmonious a way as possible whilst helping with homework, providing food, mopping up wee and not losing their rag too many times a day.

Techniques

Some of the techniques that are very likely to be used by Yolanda are the following:

- She's tried setting firm boundaries, following up with firm consequences.
- She got the kids together and they have come up with family rules.
- She has tried reward charts and praise.
- She tries to ignore the behaviour she's trying to put a stop to.
- She has tried to get in extra support.
- She sometimes shuts herself away in her bedroom to try and stop her getting too angry with her boys.
- She has told herself to try harder to be consistent even though it unsettles everybody and causes so much conflict.
- She has forced herself to give her son more attention when she is at her wit's end and just wants to escape.
- She has cried and felt ashamed of herself when she has shouted and screamed at her son to just do as he is told.
- She has kept the depth of her struggles and her shame a secret because she doesn't want anyone to know what a terrible parent she is.

Traditional: self-discipline (reward–punishment)

Approach

The fundamental point about traditional parenting advice is that understanding the deep emotional and mental impact on, and needs of, parents and carers who are struggling is a dark, gaping hole.

Techniques

Just as you might expect, from what I have outlined above, there is an absence of emphasis on the wellbeing of parents doing the parenting in this model. Therefore, the only 'technique' is a tacit expectation to try harder.

Therapeutic: self-acceptance (EBM)

Approach

Self-acceptance is going to be so crucial for Yolanda. An EBM approach would help her to be gentler and kinder to herself. It would help her to appreciate her efforts and not just critique her struggles. Self-acceptance will enable Yolanda to see herself as she really is, without fear or favour, without defence. This absence of self-criticism will mean that Yolanda won't need to defend herself against the shame. She will be able to accurately see how her parenting is going, and decide to make changes if she sees fit to do so.

Techniques

In practical terms, self-acceptance for Yolanda would look like the following:

- Giving Yolanda a space (or encouraging her to find one for herself) to express all of her frustrations, heartache and worries without fear of judgement, thus facilitating the minimization of her shame. Crucially this means that she must be allowed to be as angry and as undiplomatic about her children as she needs to be.
- Firm, clear assertions that she will not be able to parent the way that she wants to all of the time.
- Encouraging Yolanda to work out how to restore herself. This means exploring what she might need to help her to feel more able to stay regulated in her parenting. It also means developing a proactive plan about how she will achieve those things. She may need a buddy who 'gets it', regular time off

from parenting, or maybe practical support with things like cooking, cleaning, etc.

- Supporting Yolanda in understanding why she reacts as she does, helping her to truly accept her limitations and make allowances and contingency plans for them (perhaps using some of the exercises below).
- If Yolanda feels like she is feeling more acceptance of herself, she may also be able to think about trying to observe her reactions and reflect on how they have gone with fascination and curiosity, as she would do with a good, objective friend.

Let's get practical
Planning to balance our attention to needs

It is so important when we're in the middle of a tough emotional interaction with our child that we accurately pull apart what we are doing to help them and what we are doing to preserve ourselves. Both are incredibly important. It's really useful to know this information so that we can be assertive about each of those needs, and both parties can feel as well cared for as possible at a particular time.

For example, imagine a child and a parent out on a walk to the park. When they reach the park, the child begins to protest about being out of the house. This quickly escalates to loud screams and cries until the child is hysterically upset and angry. They want to be home instantly, but they have a 15-minute walk home. Below is a simple list of the actions that this parent could have taken, and whether they were directly or indirectly for the child's benefit, because those measures minimized the negative impact of their parent's stress on the child. You might find it useful as a tool to break down what has happened during one of your tricky moments with your child to help you towards self-acceptance. Remember – many things that benefit parents in such stressful scenarios also indirectly benefit their child as they prevent a parent's stress from spilling over into their relationship.

Balance of needs

Attempts to distract child.	Benefits both parent and child.
Decision to start walking home.	Benefits child.
Attempts to calm the child with empathic commentary: 'You're so upset! I know it's hard, you just want to be home.'	Benefits child.
Snapping in temper: 'Yes, I know you want to get home! You've told me a thousand times!'	Briefly benefits parent via venting frustration, justifying their efforts and highlighting the child's unreasonableness.
Ignoring child's distressed communications.	Benefits parent via attempting to block out the stressful demands. Benefits child indirectly as it is parent's attempt to not lose their temper.
Trying to help child manage the journey home and focus on home: 'We'll be there soon, just five more minutes to go.'	Benefits child.
Carrying the child.	Benefits child via regulating their feelings.
Refusing to carry the child, insisting that they walk.	Benefits parent when parent is exhausted.
Accepting child's attempts to communicate and/or manage their distress (despite the unwelcome attention it draws).	Benefits child.
Attempting to silence the child: 'Shh! You're embarrassing me!.'	Benefits parent briefly when they need to vent and express frustration.

Ways of moving from fast- to slow-thinking decision-making in the toughest moments
Grounding

Fundamentally, what we are trying to do, in moving modes of decision-making (from our Hare to our Tortoise system), is trying to shift from the most primitive areas of the brain to the pre-frontal cortex, where we can make more considered decisions. We cannot simply think ourselves into in this shift; we must talk the language of our primitive brain, and this means engaging our senses. Doing this is commonly known as 'grounding', whereby we mentally plant ourselves in the physical world to reduce our animalistic instincts, our panic, fear and rage. A quick internet search will give you countless techniques that you can sift through, and hopefully you will find something that might work for you, but a few more suggestions are listed below.

In order to simplify the idea of grounding, think sensory – anything that engages your senses and captivates your attention, even just momentarily. It can also be useful to rate your level of fear/panic/rage (whatever the overwhelming emotion might be) out of 10 before and after each grounding exercise, and then repeat if necessary.

- Take yourself to a quiet place, sit down and get comfy. Silently, to yourself, notice and name three things you can see, three things you can hear, and then three things you can smell. Then notice and name to yourself two things you can see, two you can hear and two you can smell. Then one thing you can see, one thing you can hear and one thing you can smell.
- Grab something very cold, maybe a bag of peas out of the freezer. Feel and notice the sensation and what the feeling does to your body.
- Splash your face with water and notice how this makes you feel.
- Step outside and notice the feeling of the elements on your body. Notice the wind. Feel the rain. See the shapes in the fog.
- Sing. Put on a song that makes you feel happy and sing your heart out!
- Have a shower and try to attend to the feeling of the water on your body.
- Lay down on the grass and stare at the clouds. Notice their shapes and their movement.
- Walk barefoot on the lawn or the path. Does the grass feel cool? Is the path warm under your feet?
- Bake (alone!). Get involved with the textures and smells of the ingredients and the mixture.

- List things. Come up with 10 animals that begin with 'A' or 10 countries in Europe. Although this one seems less sensory, it forces you to visualize and think methodically to engage your pre-frontal cortex.

Trying to be empathic (to yourself and your child) but accepting yourself when you fail

Usually the people who come to me are desperate for ways to stop their own rage and/or unhelpful reactions to their child, and we will try some of the techniques above. However, often more important than these techniques is the message of self-acceptance.

You will lose your temper. You will have reactions that you don't like and that are not particularly helpful for your child or their relationship with you. You will do this and so will every other adult living with a developmentally traumatized child (in fact, every person in any kind of relationship!); not because you (and all of the others) are terrible parents, but because the job you are doing tests us to the very extreme of our limits, and sometimes we will slip over the edge.

So do try these grounding techniques and sometimes they will work for you; however, do not expect them to work every time and please, please, be gentle and forgiving of yourself when they don't.

How do I accept myself and my parenting?

I hope that reading this book will have some impact on that. You have permission to let yourself off the hook on this one. Success under stress CANNOT come from self-discipline. Therefore, self-chastisement is pointless and self-acceptance is the only path to a more positive experience of parenting a developmentally traumatized child.

Sometimes parental self-acceptance has to come first, before parents can have acceptance for their child's mental and emotional states, but equally it can come afterwards. Anything that punctuates the cycle of negativity in a relationship can send it spinning in the right direction. When you start to feel able to accept your child for who they are, you may be more able to extend that acceptance to yourself and your parenting.

Either way, it is important to know that acceptance of yourself and of your child go hand in hand – the interactions between you and your child are reciprocal. It is not possible to show your child authentic acceptance unless you are really feeling some acceptance of yourself and your necessarily flawed parenting.

A great practice to support self-acceptance is mindfulness. You will be able to find lots of great resources to help with this if you look. I've included some guidance to get you started in Superpower #6: Exploring 'Why?'

Empathic self-talk

These are some simple examples of the things we might be able to say to ourselves if we are able to accept ourselves:

- 'Oh my goodness I feel angry!'
- 'Urgh, I really shouted at her then. I'm really beating myself up for it. I wish I hadn't done it. I wonder why I did?'
- 'Okay, I'm starting to feel a bit overwhelmed by all this. There's a lot going on; it's really no wonder I'm struggling.'
- 'I'm feeling like I can't cope. I want to run away.'
- 'This is awful, but this feeling will pass.'
- 'Okay, this is hard. I'm struggling because this is really, really hard, not because I'm not good enough.'

So let's take all of this back to what we know about how human brains react to stress and how our Tortoise and Hare systems are affected by stress. We need to give ourselves permission to stop criticizing ourselves and our children for our (and their) reactions to stress. I encourage you to accept that parents *and* children act on a flawed decision-making system when we are under pressure. Our Hare system will not help us much with parenting in times of extreme stress or with our impulsive reactions to emotions. So, forgiveness and readiness to repair is key.

SAFE CONTAINMENT

Introduction

The idea of rules and boundaries reaches to the very heart of traditional reward–punishment thinking. It's become such a central idea to parenting in general that it will take quite some exploration to work out how we parent without the traditional meaning of 'boundaries'. In a nutshell, the difference between the boundaries of traditional parenting and the safe containment of therapeutic parenting hinges on the different ways in which control is understood. We can frame this as the difference between *being in control of* vs. *being in control for*.

One of the biggest misconceptions about empathic or therapeutic parenting is that it is permissive. Some think that parenting therapeutically means parenting without effective use of rules. There's also a weakness in how this kind of parenting is written and spoken about. We're often not clear enough about how therapeutic parenting can be assertive and how therapeutic parents can (indeed, need to be) strong. Any critical evaluation of the idea of 'rules and boundaries' in conversations about parenting leads people to anxiously jump to the idea that parenting authority and strength are being taken away. This is most certainly not the case!

This chapter will take us through what the term 'boundaries' usually means and the impact that this approach has on developmentally traumatized children and their parents and carers. We can then open our minds to the idea of parenting using safe containment and how we can use it with our children.

Boundaries in traditional reward–punishment parenting

Clarity for parents and children

Boundaries, as they are traditionally talked about, have the benefit of assisting parents to provide their children with clarity and consistency. At their behavioural best, they set up clear expectations for everyone. Boundaries also enable everyone to know when a rule has been broken and therefore when consequences should be imposed.

The clarity that this approach facilitates can be so helpful for parents in the heat of the moment. At its best, it can take the negative emotions out of challenging interactions and/or behaviour of the child. Clarity such as this is so important for children who are primed to anticipate rejection, aggression and conflict.

There is inevitably less certainty and consistency, however, when emotions are involved. In parenting traumatized children, it is very tough to anticipate when an emotional button might get pressed. In the heat of normal, stressful trauma-parenting, behavioural expectations can get turned on their head or become too tough a goal to achieve.

Focus on behaviour

So, boundaries can be a fantastic benchmark for behaviour. Their major benefit for both children and parents, the fact that they can enable consistency and clarity, can also be their downfall when it comes to parenting developmentally traumatized children.

To fully explore the problem of applying boundaries to developmentally traumatized children, we need to fully think through how they need to be used in practice for them to be successful.

To create absolute consistency and simplicity for children, the goal in applying boundaries should be parents' uncompromising adherence to the rules. Taking a purely behavioural approach would mean that, to avoid ambiguity for children, no account should be taken of the context or the underlying emotion that drives the behaviour. The behaviour is taken at face value and if it is unacceptable, a consequence should be put in place to deter the child from behaving in that way again.

This approach can appear to work well when the child's emotional blueprint is a reasonably stable and safe one (although an empathic approach, in which parents engage with a child's inner world, will always be optimal). If a child has a core belief that he or she is safe and that his or her environment is stable and trustworthy, then boundaries are founded on solid ground. However, this is rarely the internal landscape of developmentally traumatized children.

Very often, the behaviour of children traumatized by abuse and/or neglect can be inconsistent, disorientating and sometimes downright baffling. This is because children are often dealing with emotions that make them feel exactly that way. The emotional worlds of our children can be terrifyingly unpredictable places. As a result, we are presented with an extremely tough challenge in parenting them. How do we empathize with the extreme internal circumstances our children are contending with? How do we do this whilst also offering predictable responses that will help a child to feel safe and begin to feel (and then internalize) a sense of the world as a stable and reliable place to be?

Being in control of (vs. being in control for)
Confusing force *with* strength

Reward–punishment techniques for dealing with challenging behaviour emphasize consistency – never deviating from the enforcement of the rules for fear of confusing children and diluting the power of the boundary – the logic being along the lines of, if a child doesn't know whether you will enforce the boundary, they will persist in the behaviour in order to test it.

One of the statements I sometimes hear in relation to traumatized children is that they 'are not buying into the boundaries'. Sadly, this is something often used as a rationale for a placement breaking down. This idea makes sense to a degree when we start from the default of understanding the behaviour of non-traumatized children, who do, indeed, have some trust in typical relational rules of fairness and justice. On some level, children who have not been traumatized by abuse and/or neglect do 'buy into' the boundaries placed on them. They may well object, protest and become upset when a boundary is enforced, but this is emotional and behavioural small-fry when compared to the reaction that many traumatized children have to a boundary that is imposed on a trauma-triggered behaviour.

Traumatized children can react to the imposition of boundaries in the most extreme ways, frequently with complete behavioural and emotional dysregulation and/or **dissociation**.

It is hopefully beginning to become clear that to impose boundaries (in the traditional sense) on a developmentally traumatized child, a parent or carer is almost inevitably led down a sterner, less compromising road – the more a child resists a boundary, the tougher a parent tends to become in imposing those boundaries. Parents often find themselves escalating in their need to be in control and in their need to force children to behave in a certain way. I am reminded of a parent I know who, after an exasperated few hours of asking, demanding and cajoling their adopted teenager to get into the car, eventually shouted that they would tie them up and put them in if they had to. They wouldn't have done that, of course, but frustration and the need to gain control takes us to some strange places. Nothing made a difference to that young person. Our instinct, in the cold light of day, might be to be horrified at this threat and see just how traumatizing that might have been. However, there aren't many parents of traumatized children (in fact, not many parents of non-traumatized children too) who can, hand on heart, say that they haven't ever said something extreme that they have later felt ashamed of.

Parental control is very important in both traditional and empathic, attachment-based approaches. However, the nature of that control, from the two perspectives, is very different. Reward–punishment thinking leads us down a route of taking 'control of' our children whilst an empathic approach leads us to strive to take 'control for' our children. It's the difference between how we wield our power and for whom. We will fully explore the differences between the two approaches below.

Another way of highlighting the difference in these approaches, whilst also avoiding the temptation to see an empathic approach as permissive, is to think of the difference between force and strength. A traditional approach can feel like we are forcing children to behave. An empathic approach, however, steers us away from force, but most certainly requires parental strength. That strength comprises internal fortitude but also outward confidence and assertiveness.

Impact on emotional regulation

It is so easy to dismiss challenging behaviour or rule breaks as 'just testing boundaries'; this is generally how we are encouraged to see children's behaviour. There is, indeed, from any perspective, a need for children to work out how to control their impulses. However, the language of the reward–punishment approach can encourage us to disregard what it *feels* like to be your child at the moment their behaviour crosses the line.

If we try to get inside the head of our child at the time of their rule break (and this is rarely an easy task!), we can usually see that they are struggling with some feeling or another. As covered in the book's Introduction, children (particularly developmentally traumatized children) need an adult to help them to regulate their feelings before they can do it for themselves. Even much older children need us to help them to regulate really difficult feelings. Think of a first heartbreak or major bust-ups with friends in our teenage years. The toilet training metaphor can help to illustrate how children learn to regulate their feelings. In short, this is a process that involves an attuned adult noticing the outward signs of the child's emotions, naming those feelings and acting on them to help the child internalize a sense of what each emotion means and feels like. This is just like what we do when we're reading the groin-grabbing, foot-hopping body language of a toddler who needs the loo.

When our children come to us with sadness, loneliness and tears, it is relatively easy for our empathy to kick in. However, when they come to us with annoyance, rage or sheer uncooperativeness and all the frustration, shouting, hitting and destructiveness that can come with it, our empathy invariably gets overwhelmed by our own anger and fear. We typically turn to reward–punishment-based behaviour management in an attempt to make those unbearable feelings stop– quickly. The biggest hurdle in using EBM (or therapeutic parenting) is to truly recognize that negative emotions (those that invade with fury and fight) need just as much empathy as those that travel via sadness and sobbing.

So, when we think in terms of rules and boundaries, it is much harder to hold in mind how much of a struggle our children go through with their rage and fear-based emotions. When we apply the consistent, somewhat cold, logic of reward–punishment thinking at these times, we fail to regulate our children. This technique can, in fact, cause our children's emotions to escalate. In addition, they do not get the experience that they so badly need, of having their feelings calmed and understood. When we apply boundaries without safe containment, we are effectively saying to children who already aren't coping, 'just cope better' or there'll be consequences. We do that whilst simultaneously declining the opportunity to support them in developing their ability to cope better. Put simply, by thinking about boundaries, rather than safe containment, we make the problem of emotional regulation, and therefore behavioural outbursts, worse and more likely to happen again in the future.

Boundaries as safe containment

Containment in this context refers to the psychological phenomenon rather than the idea of 'holding something in'. Psychological containment is the process by which an adult hears and internalizes the distress of a baby (or child), regulates the feeling that is passed to them and can then send back verbal and non-verbal messages that the emotion can be coped with. Over time that baby learns that their feelings are manageable – initially, that their feelings are manageable to someone else, but eventually they internalize the idea that emotions can be contained and regulated within themselves and that they can cope.

Safe containment is therefore the idea of keeping children safe from being overwhelmed by their own feelings (and ours). We do this by making sense of feelings *for* children and by simply experiencing their world with them. In the context of challenging behaviour, children also require us to process their behaviour by making sense of the feelings that cause it. They require us to help them to behave well via processing their emotions (just as we do for babies). In doing this we are protecting them from their own trauma reactions as well as teaching them how to behave in a way that makes life happier for all concerned. Children's trauma reactions can come to define how they see themselves and how they are seen by others; for example, aggressive, needy, chaotic or simply 'naughty'. There is a danger of creating a self-fulfilling prophecy for our children, where their trauma behaviour defines who they are in the eyes of others and indeed in their own eyes. If we are to avoid this, we need to take the route of safe containment of emotions and empathic understanding of behaviour rather than applying uncompromising, inflexible adherence to boundaries.

Child experiences catastrophic anxiety and terror

Child cries

Parent briefly becomes anxious too

BUT

Manages their own emotions quite quickly; the adult can cope with it

Child's emotions are regulated

Adult soothes and thus communicates, verbally and non-verbally, that they recognize the feeling and it will be okay

'I will keep you safe from being someone who is destructive'

'I will keep you safe'

Over time, when the child experiences this on most occasions (it does not need to be all of the time), they acquire the capacity, through developing neural networks, to regulate their own emotions

'I will keep you from disliking yourself'

Safe containment

'Strong pair of arms' metaphor

Think of safe containment as a strong pair of loving arms. It is our job to protect our children from the harm their own behaviour may do them as well as others. This may occasionally mean the physical harm they may do to themselves, but much more frequently it is emotional damage they do to themselves when their trauma invites relationships that are defined by aggression or conditional affection, for example. Safe containment can also help keep children safe from ending up with a self-image that is based on negative views about themselves: 'I hurt people', 'I make people stop loving me', etc.

To help illustrate safe containment as an alternative to boundary setting, it can be helpful to think about the way we instinctively support babies when they express negative emotions.

 ## ERICA AND LEXI

When trying to get her 11-month-old daughter to sleep, Erica lies on her bed with her baby, Lexi, in the crook of her arm, cuddled up close. Lexi is not keen to go to sleep and she moves suddenly, as if to look behind her and resist her mum's attempts to get her to sleep. Both Erica and Lexi are irritated. Erica moves reflexively and pulls Lexi tight to prevent her from falling off the edge of the bed. This is not the most comfortable of reactions for Lexi; it jolts her body and shocks her. She cries. Despite Lexi's shock and fear, how deeply comforting must it be for Lexi to react through irritation but know she's safely held and won't be allowed to fall off the bed. Imagine the alternative: if Erica gives up her firm hold and Lexi's irritation results in her coming to harm. Erica persists in her soothing (despite her own frustration), and eventually Lexi is able to overcome her irritation and fear, relax, and fall fast asleep.

Being in control for

There is certainly a need for parental control in relation to challenging behaviour. It is not in any way helpful for parents to not have control when they are taking an empathic approach. However, a traditional approach leads us to feel that we must have 'control of' our children's behaviour – in many cases, control of our children in their entirety. When we shift towards an empathic approach, we take a more collaborative perspective. It then becomes more relevant to talk about parents being in *control for* rather than being in *control of*.

The need for adults to have control in relation to themselves

Before any adult can contemplate the idea of taking an empathic approach to the challenging behaviour of their child, there is first a need to focus our attention inwards. In order to cope with the emotional load of therapeutic parenting, particularly at times we're empathizing with something that presses all of our buttons, it is important for adults to focus on self-acceptance first and then self-regulation whenever it is possible (see Superpower #1: Parental Self-Acceptance).

Boundary setting can often become disconnecting and punitive when parents and carers feel overwhelmed by the emotions their child is bringing them via their behaviour. It is pretty much impossible to be empathic and safely containing when we are not regulated ourselves.[40, 41] It is much more important for us to have as much control of ourselves (through self-acceptance and regulation) as possible so that we can exercise control for our children.

When we are not regulated, the control centre of our brains (our executive functions) are impaired, and our Hare decision-making system is even more dominant than usual (see Superpower #1: Parental Self-Acceptance and earlier in this chapter). We make reflex decisions that are not consistent with how we would like to parent and how we need to parent our developmentally traumatized children. In a dysregulated state we make decisions about our parenting that, for all the reasons discussed above, will be behaviour-focused, disconnecting and not safely containing for our children.

The need for adult control in relation to children's behaviour

Early in this chapter, we have already begun to explore why EBM doesn't mean being permissive. However, it is important to elaborate on this further.

Many looked-after and adopted children have come from neglectful or emotionally harmful situations. Often this means that they were left alone, physically and/or emotionally, to deal with more than they were able to. One consequence of this is that their emotional regulation systems can fail to develop as well as they might. With no one to regulate children's feelings and behaviours, they cannot internalize the process for themselves. Another consequence for our children is that they may have been left to manage tremendous amounts of responsibility, for themselves, their siblings and possibly their parents. Many have been left with no safe, predictable limits placed on their behaviour – no boundaries. Combining these two elements leaves children with no safe containment, a feeling that their emotions are manageable.

The lack of safe containment is frightening for any child. It is therefore crucial that we don't, through attempts to be empathic about the causes of behaviour, recreate this lack of safety. We must avoid the replication of children's trauma experiences by not giving them unmanageable, excessive control (and therefore responsibility). Parenting developmentally traumatized children, using either permissive or punitive approaches, can lead to the replication of their early trauma experiences.

Focus on emotion

The central focus of safe containment is on emotion. When confronted with a behavioural issue, particularly when it is extreme and difficult, our goal is to look through the behaviour and go eyeball to eyeball with the emotion behind it. A good level of attunement to your child is very helpful when looking for these disguised emotions, but it won't be enough to get it right every time. For example, a 7-year-old who is screaming and kicking you because you have told them that it's bedtime is showing rage, but to us that rage doesn't make sense. Going to bed isn't that bad after all! So we need to stop trying to apply behavioural cause–effect thinking. To get to the sense of this, we need to accept emotions as facts rather than right or wrong, or indeed worrying that they are manipulations. We can use them as the foundation for understanding our children. We can read the emotion via the behaviour: 'This child is experiencing an emotion that causes this behaviour' – fact. 'What emotion could cause a child to do this?' – in this case, it's likely to be fear. The thoughts that come so quickly afterwards about why the child feels frightened may be useful later, but in the moment all you need is the emotion or even a good guess at it. The 'Let's get practical' strategies section (see below) will go into more detail about how to apply this technique.

This process is extraordinarily challenging, particularly in the heat of the moment, so please don't beat yourself up when you forget, or it goes wrong, or it just feels like the wrong approach and you hear yourself saying 'I'm not letting him get away with it', 'She's got to learn that there are consequences', etc.

As detailed above, focusing purely on behaviour has some major downsides. Emotionally, for example, it may leave the child with fear that overwhelms them; and behaviourally, we can inadvertently make the behaviour worse by leaving children alone with the frightening emotion that drives that behaviour. The aim is to focus on emotion and to place the idea of behavioural management firmly in the periphery. In doing this we can join our child in their distress and their self-sabotaging behaviours, and navigate through it with them.

In reaching for emotion first we are more likely to dissolve our child's defences and be allowed into their inner world, where the answers lie. If we are present and available to respond to (and regulate) our child's most challenging emotions, just as we would with a baby, then we start to have a positive impact on our child's ability to regulate their feelings for themselves. It's this emotional regulation that, over time, enables a child to regulate their behaviour.

IMPORTANT NOTE! When you are doing this successfully, it's very likely you won't see the progress you are indeed making. It often takes someone from the outside to notice progress in emotional regulation, but progress in this skill is a big deal: 'Jack managed to keep hold of his temper today', 'Keisha went to hit me today but stopped herself'. Look out for these comments from others and try hard to observe them for yourself. They are signs that children are regulating big emotions and engaging the pre-frontal cortex of their brains. If they couldn't do these things and now they can, it's because you have helped them to; it's your and your child's win, and you should make sure you both feel proud of it!

Let's run through the process of traditional reward–punishment thinking when a child's behaviour is challenging, when it crosses a boundary and we might impose a consequence. To clarify exactly how the traditional and EBM approaches and techniques may be similar or different, we will explore what might be a textbook response to a real-life scenario. We will also look at a realistic version of what our Hare decision-making might lead us to do, that is, what might realistically, spontaneously happen. These scenarios will hopefully help us to explore and demonstrate what EBM is all about (and what it isn't).

✸ KAI AND JANE

Kai, a 9-year-old boy, lives with his adoptive mum, Jane. After a stressful day at school, Kai is eating his dinner. After finishing his dessert, Kai throws his bowl on the floor and breaks it after he is told that he cannot have more ice cream.

Reality: the exhausted Hare	Traditional: boundaries	Therapeutic: self-containment
✕	✕	✓
(Unpredictable)	(Not trauma-informed)	(Trauma-informed)

Comparison of approaches

Reality: the exhausted Hare
Approach

In the book's Introduction and Superpower #1: Parental Self-Acceptance, we explored the idea of slow and rational Tortoise decision-making vs. automatic and impulsive Hare decision-making. We know from research that the majority of our decisions are made via our Hare system, quickly and automatically. Despite what we tell ourselves, parenting is mostly winging it, making decisions on the hoof, and then making sense of why we did it later. Often the best we can do is accept what we've done and why, and try to squeeze in some better thought through Tortoise decisions where we can.

The exhausted Hare 'approach' is the way parenting often gets done, particularly by parents and carers trying their hardest to look after challenging, developmentally traumatized children. This is not what any of us would necessarily consider to be the ideal way of doing things, but, given the stresses and strains of this kind of 'superparenting', it's real and sometimes can be quite 'good enough'.

The exhausted Hare can only wryly be called an 'approach', as it's not really as organized as the word suggests. The overarching parenting drive of the exhausted Hare is to get their home running in as harmonious a way as possible whilst helping with homework, providing food, mopping up wee and not losing their rag too many times a day.

Specifically, in relation to setting boundaries, the exhausted Hare would deal with Kai by using the techniques that come to mind most quickly and are the most economical in their use of resources from her poor tired brain.

Techniques

The techniques most likely to be used are any number of the following:

- Trying to make chaotic behaviour make sense: 'Why on earth did you do that?!'
- Keeping everyone safe: 'Keep out of the way, you're going to tread on the broken pieces.'
- Stating the bleeding obvious: 'You've just thrown one of my bowls!'
- Staying as calm as possible: 'Go upstairs now!' (Before I lose my reason.)
- Wondering what on earth to do: (Thinking, if not saying) 'What on earth am I going to do with him?'
- Trying to feel in control by applying consequences, reparation, justice, something! (ANYTHING!): 'Right, get back down here and help me clear this mess up', 'You certainly won't be having any more ice cream this week', 'I've had enough of this, Kai!'
- Debriefing some time later: 'Why on earth did you throw that bowl earlier? I've just about had enough of this, Kai! You can't behave like that. You know you can't have too much ice cream. You could have hurt someone!'

Traditional: boundaries (reward–punishment)
Approach

The traditional approach to this behaviour would be to focus on the behaviour alone, to isolate the bowl-breaking behaviour. This behaviour would be seen as a result of the child not having fully internalized the idea that behaviours have consequences. According to this approach the child should be helped to understand that behaviours have consequences by implementing a sanction that the child will not like. This should cause the child to learn that the next time he is tempted to behave aggressively or destructively, he should not, otherwise he will have to suffer another consequence.

The ideal process for this approach would be for the adult to calmly explain that the behaviour is not acceptable, that the child could have hurt someone, and then what the consequence for his behaviour will be. If the child were to resist that consequence, the adult would be encouraged to bring in further, more severe, consequences, or to physically impose the consequence. This is very much 'being in control *of*'.

Techniques

There are any number of specific rewards and punishments that could be used as a consequence for Kai's behaviour. The key message from this approach is that the boundary must be enforced, and the consequence must be motivational: we have to do something that the child will not like and will try to avoid in the future. Some options would be:

- Kai should be told that throwing the bowl is unacceptable.
- There should be minimal conversation with Kai at the time of the event to minimize hostility but also to prevent reinforcing the behaviour if Kai is 'just attention-seeking'.
- Kai could be put in time out in his bedroom for nine minutes (one minute for every year of his life).
- Kai might not be allowed to have ice cream again for a week.
- Kai might be given a reward chart. Every day he isn't physically aggressive, he gets a sticker or 20p towards his weekly pocket money.

As we have discussed above, often with developmentally traumatized children these techniques will cause an escalation of the aggression and hostility. They will certainly do nothing to help Kai to understand his own outburst, find a way out of his shame or regulate his feelings and therefore his behaviour in the future.

Therapeutic: safe containment (EBM)
Approach
The therapeutic approach to Kai's behaviour would start with ourselves. How did the bowl throwing make us feel? Are we feeling regulated? Are we bordering on losing our temper? Are we emotionally preoccupied or feeling calm and rational?

Only when we've worked out our own emotional state can we place any expectation on ourselves to deal therapeutically with our child's. If we're not feeling regulated, then our reaction will have already happened for good or for bad, and we can evaluate it and, if necessary, repair its effects later.

Once we're regulated, we can begin to consider Kai's behaviour in the context of his internal world. The goal would be to help Kai to regulate the emotion that caused the behaviour and then help him to understand why, from an emotional perspective, he broke the bowl – for example, 'You were so cross!' Once Kai is calmer (this may be minutes, hours or days later), the adult taking an EBM perspective would help Kai to protect and enhance his self-esteem and the relationships that may have been damaged by his behaviour. It's important to reiterate that in order for the adult to execute this approach, they will need to be gentle with themselves, and may need to take some time after the event to deal with their own difficult feelings about the child's behaviour.

Techniques
We'll cover the full gamut of EBM techniques for safe containment in the next section, but let's first deal with how we could address Kai's behaviour using a safe containment approach. There are several ways we could therapeutically approach Kai's bowl throwing, and this is just one.

First, we must start with our poor exhausted Hare. Kai's adoptive mum, Jane, has already set herself up with a way to regulate her emotions in times of stress. She talks regularly with her mum who 'gets it'. Her mum gets that Jane needs to vent without judgement and that, despite how furious she gets with Kai at times, she wants to parent him in an empathic way and not try to discipline him out of feeling and behaving the way he does. Jane's mum has been well versed in how to support Jane to do it her way. Jane also uses some grounding techniques and some empathic self-talk (first covered in Superpower #1: Parental Self-Acceptance).

Jane is having a good day overall and so she can slip into some safe containment techniques for Kai. She holds in mind that Kai needs her to be in control, but that anger will cause him to kick off even more.

- Jane starts with safety. She places herself between the broken bowl and the children and sweeps the pieces up. Kai is reluctant to move, so she explains calmly that it's not safe for him to be in the kitchen and that she's not angry, and gently ushers him into the lounge.

- Jane then moves to empathic commentary to regulate Kai's feelings. She says 'You're so cross with me!' Then later, 'I'm so sorry I couldn't let you have more ice cream. I understand that it makes you cross.' She says this or variations of it over and over again for about half an hour whilst Kai protests (but he isn't aggressive). She tries to give him as much one-to-one attention during this time as she can, but also has to get on with helping her daughter with her spellings.

- Jane also uses a natural consequence. She is very clear with Kai that she's sad that it happened and that she can't let him use the breakable crockery until they can work out what happened and how she can help Kai with the feelings that caused him to break the bowl.

- Jane tries to gauge when Kai is feeling more regulated and tries being playful: 'How's my poor floor doing?' she says, stroking where the bowl hit and giving Kai a wink. If Kai wasn't as regulated as she thought, he may well start shouting again about wanting more ice cream.

- Jane takes a deep breath and starts from the beginning again.

- This time she feels that Kai is regulated enough to be able to handle some contact, so she squeezes his shoulder.

- Kai moves on to some other topic and the family's evening continues. WIN!

- The next day Kai seems calm and well regulated. Jane discusses reparation to help Kai to feel that he can let go of his shame: 'What do you think is a fair way to make things better for throwing the bowl, Kai?' They talk about it and agree that he'll take the bagged-up broken pieces to the wheelie bin. He's not keen on the idea but eventually they agree that he'll use his pocket money to buy another bowl. She is careful not to shame Kai. Her purpose in helping him find a way to repair is so that he can know that he's done his bit to contribute to getting the relationship back on track and in the hope he can let the whole incident go. She feels proud of him and pleased for him that he has been able to accept her parenting, and shows him so.
- They go out together to buy the new bowl. Jane sets a celebratory mood: 'Look what we've achieved together.'

We will now elaborate on the techniques that you can use when employing a safe containment approach, and how they make sense from an empathic perspective.

Let's get practical
Self-regulation

First and foremost, when using safe containment, the techniques need to start with *you*. Unless you are feeling safely contained and regulated, then being calm and empathic for your child is going to be so much tougher and far more likely to go wrong. For that reason, amongst others, you might not feel able in the moment to do this for your child. The goal is to plan and to try and not beat yourself up on the occasions it goes wrong.

There are some ideas for self-regulation activities below, but really the task is to work out what regulates you. We are all different, and what keeps one person calm and in control of their emotions may not work for another.

In Superpower #1: Parental Self-Acceptance there is quite a lot of detail on grounding, which is a good self-regulation technique. Here are a few other ideas.

The first and most important thing is to not allow yourself to be on your own with the stress of raising a developmentally traumatized child. The best advice I can give to any 'superparent' is to set up a buddy system. We all need someone who 'gets it', someone who understands that developmentally traumatized children can struggle with elements of their behaviour and how your child struggles specifically. You also need your buddy to 'get' how you struggle with your child, the particular things that press your buttons. It's crucial that this person has that empathic string to their bow and won't judge you when you need to rant or at times when you (inevitably) aren't empathic to your child. You also need someone who won't judge your child, someone who gets that their behaviour won't be helped by condemnation, shame or punishment. Your buddy needs to be someone who has empathy for you and your child and won't condemn either of you when you struggle.

'Please put on your own oxygen mask before assisting others'

Self-care is crucial to being able to regulate your emotions and therefore deal with your child's challenging feelings. On this score you know much better than I do what works for you: exercise, wine, a meal out with friends, regular time on your own to watch soaps, wine, listening to music, a bath, wine. Whatever it is, it requires prioritizing in your family, and you are likely to need support in order to do it. It's not instinctive to look after ourselves first, but it is anything but self-indulgent. If we don't take this step, we very quickly become no good to anyone.

Regulating your child

Once we are in a good-enough, regulated-enough state, we can move on to thinking about trying to regulate our child when they are in the middle of an outburst that might invite us to use boundaries and consequences.

Understanding 'why?': emotional commentary

Commentating on emotions calmly and empathically is one of the most powerful techniques there is when it comes to dealing with the behaviour of children traumatized by abuse and neglect.

The emotional commentary technique is, in short, a way of commentating on your child's emotion (not behaviour or thought) without judgement or inflection from your own emotions. You can see above in our example that Jane does this with Kai. She says, with care and empathy, and with the same emotional energy that Kai is displaying, 'You're so cross with me!' She then elaborates a little when the time is right: 'I'm so sorry I couldn't let you have more ice cream. I understand that it makes you cross.'

Emotional commentary is powerful because it shows your child that you can look past behaviour and see 'why'. The internal worlds of our children are often so confused and confusing that someone really seeing past our negative impulses to what emotions are driving us in any given moment is incredibly calming. We are all so used to being condemned, blamed and fought against when our demons turn to negative behaviour, that when someone compassionately sees through it to our vulnerability and the good reasons why, we can't help but feel soothed. There is no longer anything to fight against, so the conflict simply evaporates.

Examples of empathic commentary for safe containment include:

- 'You're so angry right now!'
- 'Something so huge is going on for you that you need to show me how bad it is.'
- 'Gosh, you really are going through something to make you do something so dangerous. I want to try and help.'
- 'You're struggling and I want to help. I can't let you hurt yourself or anyone else.'
- 'I'm so sorry that your feelings have got so big you're struggling to cope with them. I'm going to try my best to help.'

Playfulness

Well-timed playfulness and silliness can also be fantastic at helping to regulate your child. How to time it? Well, that seems to be something of a mysterious art that relies on attunement. Usually, we need to look for those moments where children are continuing conflict because they are backed into an emotional cul-de-sac and we have a hunch that if they could get out without 'losing', they would. At these times you could try being daft. It may not work and if not, just as Jane does above, you can try other things and go for the silliness again later.

As for what playfulness or silliness looks like, generally it's taking a risk to make yourself look silly or have eyes rolled at you (or be sworn at). It's important to judge it so that your silliness doesn't feel mocking to your child, and this can be quite a fine line. Playfulness like this needs to be inclusive. In our example Jane gives Kai a wink so that he knows he's being included in the silliness. I've given a few examples below, but any number of things could work – anything that makes you both smile or even laugh has a chance of working. Even an eye roll can be a sign of reconnection.

I find toilet humour often works well – anything that undercuts the seriousness of a situation. In the midst of conflict with her teenage foster daughter, Sharon would often wait for a break in hostilities, carry on going about her business making dinner, chatting to the other children, etc., and then make a point of bending down to get something out of a low cupboard and blowing the largest, most exaggerated raspberry she could muster. She would then stand up with bulging eyes and faux embarrassment. It would often get a smile and a shake of the head from her foster daughter, maybe accompanied by an 'Oh my God you're disgusting!' but they both then knew that they could move on.

Sal and his 5-year-old adopted daughter would often get into conflict when it came to getting her out of the door for school. Rather than opting to put a boundary in place, which he had found just escalated the distress for both of them, he used silliness to break the tension and regulate her mood. He would elaborately and exaggeratedly try to put her coat on himself as they were getting ready to go out. He would stand with one hand just poking through her tiny purple puffer jacket, pretending to get really cross with himself because he couldn't seem to get his coat on. It was only when his daughter would say 'No, Daddy, that's MY jacket' that he would 'realize' and then ask her to show him which coat was his.

Physical contact

This is another technique that requires some discretion. Sometimes touching a child, when they're doing something for which they might expect boundary setting, is the last thing you should do as it may escalate things. However, some children who are more on the upset than angry side of things may be calmed by a gentle touch to the shoulder or an affectionate stroke of the hair. When you're tuned in to your child, you will know whether this is a technique worth trying. If it doesn't go well, you can try something else and come back to it another time.

Immediate intervention

It's a bit of an overstatement to call this one a technique, to be honest, but there are techniques that go alongside it to make it more empathic.

Sometimes your children will do something that you need to stop straightaway. Make sure you are clear with yourself about what these occasions are, though. This is not just an excuse to physically intervene in some behaviour you just don't like. These occasions are usually centred round dangerous or destructive behaviours; for example, a child who refuses to hold your hand by a busy road, or a teenager who is manhandling their sibling so roughly that you're worried someone will get hurt.

Beginning statements with a regretful but assertive 'I can't let you...' helps tremendously in these situations to get us in a safe containment rather than boundaries mindset. We are not saying, 'I'm not going to let you...' We are kindly and assertively saying (without necessarily saying out loud), 'If I let you carry on, I will not be keeping you safe, so I can't let you continue to do that.'

Alongside 'I can't...' it can also be useful to use empathic commentary about the emotional effects that your assertiveness may cause: 'I'm sorry I have to physically stop you, I know it might make you angrier in that moment but I can't let you carry on play-fighting like that with your brother – it's not safe.'

Natural consequences

Picking your battles carefully is very important when there are potentially quite a few! If not, it can feel like the whole of family life is conflict and unhappiness. See Superpower #7: Behavioural Change vs. Emotional Acceptance for a more thorough exploration of this issue.

Another way to minimize the conflict and therefore disconnection involved in daily interactions with our children is to use natural consequences. Natural consequences also begin the process of children developing reflective capacity on their own behaviour whilst minimizing the shame or disconnection of someone artificially imposing a consequence.

A natural consequence is simply not preventing the negative effects of a behaviour. For example, if a teenager doesn't tidy their room, then they will not be able to find their things when they want them. This means that the adult should not step in and find things when they are needed or wanted. However, we can still accept that it is genuinely difficult to do for some reason and be empathic to our child when they struggle as a result.

Another example of a natural consequence would be that a child who refuses the meal or selection of meals on offer would not be given extra choices (until the next meal or snack). This one should be used very selectively and is not recommended for children for whom food is a part of their trauma history. It is important with this technique to reiterate, as many times as necessary: 'The food we agreed on is still available. I don't ever want you to feel hungry!' Again, acceptance of the difficulty with the structure of mealtimes and empathy with the lack of control are very important to maintain connection.

It is best to discuss and explain the use of natural consequences with your child before you introduce it. 'I can't…' statements are useful in this context too when using a safe containment approach: 'I can't let us fall out every mealtime, our relationship is too important, so let's try this way instead.'; 'I get annoyed and worried about being able to replace things when you lose them and I have to find them and I can't let that happen to our relationship, it's too precious!'

Reparation

One of the most difficult things for developmentally traumatized children and young people to deal with in relation to their behaviour is the impact it has on their self-image and their relationships. It is therefore important that children be enabled to minimize their shame and repair their relationships when their negative emotions have damaged these things.

Reparation is a fantastic way to do this. The issue of reparation should be brought up with the child when the emotional heat of an event has dissipated. To borrow a phrase from Non-Violent Resistance (NVR) Therapy, we need to strike when the iron is cold.[42] This ensures that the child has as much distance from the shame and fall-out of the event as possible. Then the topic of reparation can be introduced as a way of making things feel better for them and for the other person who was negatively affected by the behaviour.

A child who breaks their friend's toy could be helped to think about how the event has affected them and their friend and their relationship (whilst still minimizing shame), and then the parent and child could come up with a form of reparation together. It may be that the child contributes to buying a replacement toy with their pocket money or that the parent will buy the replacement but the child will make a card to say sorry.

A young person who trashes their room could be helped to understand the impact of doing so on themselves and on their parent or siblings. This would only happen after an adult has empathically helped the angry child to make sense of why they did it and acknowledged how distressed they must have been to have done it. They could then, for example, be helped to find a way to apologize or help the sibling feel less frightened about the volatile behaviour.

'I can't...' statements can be useful when using reparation too; for example: 'I can't allow you to sabotage your relationships with me and your brother so I want to try and help you to mend them.' 'I can't allow you to carry on feeling this bad about what happened. Let's find a productive way out of that feeling.'

CELEBRATION

Introduction

Traditionally and instinctively, when our children do something 'good', we want to praise them for it. Most of us would assume that there can't be anything bad about praise; and with some slight changes in thinking, maybe, on the whole, there isn't. Remember, this book is not about throwing away all of our strategies, but by the end of this chapter you might see praise slightly differently. You may also opt to still do something very similar to 'praising' your child, but it may well have a different emphasis and a greater power to improve the relationship between you and your child.

It might be that you use praise in a way that is entirely consistent with how we will come to know celebration in this chapter, as a chance to connect and celebrate with your child. However, using praise as a strategy doesn't *necessarily* have that joyful, connecting component that celebrating with them does.

Praise in reward–punishment thinking

There are three ways in which behaviour can be changed with reward–punishment thinking: positive reinforcement (rewards for good behaviour, sticker charts, etc.), negative reinforcement (escaping bad conditions) and punishment (any type of 'consequence', such as grounding, time out, etc.).

Praise is a positive reinforcer in traditional reward–punishment models. It is a technique that we apply when we see behaviour we like, to make it more likely to occur again. It is a way of shaping the behaviour of a child and making it 'better' in our eyes. Let's go back to the book's Introduction and the origins of reward–punishment thinking. It was developed as a strategy to control behaviour, and was trialled and tested with animals. Reinforcers and punishments were designed to be applied almost robotically, and the quality of the relationship in which they occurred was entirely beside the point. The strategic use of praise is just one example of a reward approach in parenting; we'll cover rewards in their entirety in Superpower #9: Building Motivation and Hope.

Focus on behaviour

Talking about praise as a way of managing the behaviour of developmentally traumatized children leads us to use it coldly, in a transactional way: 'If you do something good, in return you'll be praised.' It focuses us on what our children get materially from our relationship with them. This approach also leads us to focus rather narrowly on behaviour and ignore the emotional causes of behaviour and the emotive nature of parenting, particularly parenting a child traumatized by abuse and/or neglect. It also misses the connectedness and interactional nature of our relationships with our children. It doesn't take into account how our children's behaviour makes us feel. When we care for or love a child, their success, achievements and happiness make us proud and happy – it makes us want to celebrate with them!

The mechanistic way of 'using' praise to manage behaviour is not generally how parents use praise in the real world, but it is what is meant when we are encouraged to use it as a strategy in parenting. Rather than a cold application of a strategy, the times when parents and carers praise their children are emotional, heart-warming experiences for parents and children alike. It is this reality of praise that has the power when we are looking from a therapeutic parenting or EBM perspective. When praise feels joyful and connecting for parents and their children, parents are not just applying a technique; they are feeling happy together, celebrating something that makes everybody feel good.

Conditional connection

As we have discussed, the real-life way in which praise is used typically involves a great deal of celebration and connection between parents and their children. However, when praise (and the shared joy and connection that comes with it) is strictly contingent on 'good' behaviour, this implies that the connection disappears when behaviour is not so desirable. In this way, a reward–punishment approach to praise conveys conditional love. However, it is unconditional love that facilitates positive connection, relational security and high self-esteem.

It is essential to the success of praise as a traditional parenting technique that it can be withdrawn when there is undesirable behaviour. This is, of course, the same for all rewards. They are only effective when they are very directly linked to the behaviour that we are seeking to encourage.

The withdrawal of the joyful connection that is integral to celebration can be a significant problem for our children as it is the connection to us that helps them to regulate and reduce their levels of shame. Conversely, disconnection and the consequent emotional dysregulation and increase in shame are more likely to trigger 'bad' behaviour. We can therefore see that using praise as a strategy can become a problem when the powerful potential of connection is withdrawn. The withdrawal of praise when behaviour is 'bad' can actually cause worse behaviour because the disconnection and sense of evaluation cause more challenging emotional states that are incompatible with reciprocal social engagement.[43, 44]

What do we mean by celebration?

Emotional honesty

When we are tuned in to how our child feels and we are regulated enough to be empathic, celebration is instinctive. It's important to free ourselves up to be emotionally honest in our interactions with our children when behaviour is challenging *and* when things are going well. It's the latter that we're focusing on in this chapter. Traditional reward–punishment-based parenting often encourages us to take emotion out of our parenting. Techniques like praise, consistency and consequences rely on unemotional, objective application of the strategies. This can be useful if parents' emotions are uncontained, which, let's be honest, they very often can be when we're dealing with early trauma. However, when we take emotion away, we encourage disconnection, which is the opposite of what developmentally traumatized children need. In the case of positive behaviour, keeping ourselves emotionally regulated is easier, so it is much less fraught to think about being emotionally honest in these good times.

Focus on connection and emotion

When we think of celebration as part of an EBM approach, we are giving ourselves permission to go with how we feel and connect with our child via our shared emotion. We abandon the traditional focus on behaviour and focus instead on emotion. We ask ourselves (mostly instinctively and unconsciously), 'What is my child feeling right now?' And then we notice how we are feeling in response. We don't need to check with ourselves, 'Should I be encouraging this?' We can follow our feelings, throw caution to the wind and enjoy good times when they pop up.

Celebration requires us to feel something positive with another person. When we genuinely feel pleasure with another person, we can't help but celebrate, from the subtleties of a shared smile to a more obvious jumping squeal and hug. Often when we focus on celebration over praise the difference is defined by who leads the emotional tone. In praise it is commonly the adult who leads – even if a child is not feeling particularly good about something they've done but an adult wants to reinforce it, they will praise the child for doing something they consider to be 'good'. Going with a celebratory approach sometimes means following the child's emotional lead, reading the child's emotion first and then allowing it to impact on you: 'I feel good because you feel good.' However, we can also focus on being honest about our own emotions, and when we feel proud or excited about some element of our relationship with our child, we can get in touch with it and show it! We may need to test our child's reaction to that kind of celebration, but sometimes children can breezily be swept along in the joy.

Sharing joy, success, pride and excitement is a sure-fire way to connect with your child and to engage them in positive behaviour.

How celebration impacts on behaviour

As we have discussed in the previous section, praise used as a traditional parenting technique to reward 'good' behaviour can bring celebration and connection with it, but when the praise stops, this can cause disconnection and the emotional (and therefore behavioural) challenges that come with it. It unintentionally teaches vulnerable, emotionally fragile children that if we don't like their behaviour (and any distressing emotion that causes it), we will disconnect from them. They then lose the person who can help them to regulate themselves and their behaviour and feel good about themselves. This invariably creates the challenging behaviour we are so desperate to avoid.

Celebration, on the other hand, when used in tandem with emotional regulation (see also Superpower #2: Safe Containment) encourages connection regardless of behaviour – this approach does not punish with our absence or via disconnection from us. The very act of connecting with a child makes them more likely to want to invest in their relationship with us and more likely to behave in a collaborative, cooperative way, that is, they are more likely to behave 'better'. This is because they feel safer, better understood and more hopeful that they could feel good about their relationship with their parents or carers and ultimately about themselves. However, in reality, this journey can be a long (and sometimes challenging) one.

Reinforcement as a by-product

Using reward–punishment language, we can say that celebrating success and feeling joy or pride *with* our children reinforces the behaviour that caused it.

Using EBM language, we would say that parents and children sharing heart-warming, emotional experiences with one another is more likely to enable a child to invest trust in their parent. This happens via a parent or carer appreciating a child's victory over a struggle and then sharing their joy that they have succeeded.

This is all whilst simultaneously learning that their parent or carer won't judge them for the times when they have struggled. There is a sense that both the victory and the struggle are experienced between parent and child together as a joint endeavour. Therefore, any negative experience, that might otherwise be felt to be a failure or some internal flaw, could not be judged as 'belonging' to the child.

Celebration can also mean both parent and child feel great about the same thing, but there is no attempt to reinforce the behaviour that caused it. It can be about connecting and feeling good together for its own sake. For example, imagine a parent and a 5-year-old child sitting together across a dinner table. The adult notices that the child is making fish faces and giggling. The parent may well join in the silly mood, make eye contact with their child, and start the same fish impressions with a similar grin on their face. This develops into a reciprocal game whereby the child pulls the fish face and the adult copies, then the child does it in an even more exaggerated way and the adult even more so. Both parent and child are celebrating a happy mood together, completely non-verbally. The initial fish face from the child is not something that a parent would praise, but the pleasure becomes mutually rewarding and connecting.

Let's think through the process when children do something that is considered a desirable behaviour and are pleased with themselves. To clarify exactly how the traditional and EBM approaches and techniques may be similar or different, we will explore what might be a textbook response to a real-life scenario. This will help us to explore what EBM is all about (and what it isn't). As well as looking at what each of the approaches would have us aspire to, we will also explore a more real-life example of how our exhausted Hare might react.

✸ CHARLIE, DEAN AND PAULA

Charlie, a 15-year-old girl, comes home from school to her foster parents, Dean and Paula. She's acting a little strangely, fidgeting, and a bit embarrassed, but full of 'I don't care' bravado. She throws a school workbook on the kitchen table, not something she would usually do. 'What's up love? How did the Geography test go?' Paula asks.

'Nothing. You gonna look in the book or what?' Charlie responds in a surly way. Charlie goes upstairs to her bedroom. When Paula looks in Charlie's workbook, she finds that Charlie has got 21 out of 40 on her Geography test and Mr Wright, her teacher, has written 'Well done, Charlie, you got all the capital cities!'

Reality: the exhausted Hare	Traditional: praise	Therapeutic: celebration
✗	✗	✓
(Unpredictable)	(Not trauma-informed)	(Trauma-informed)

Comparison of approaches

Reality: the exhausted Hare
Approach
Before we dive into how traditional and then therapeutic or EBM approaches would recommend that we respond to Charlie, let's do a quick reality check with our poor exhausted Hare. Remember, this relates back to the Hare decision-making system, the impulsive, quick way we generally make decisions, particularly when we are stressed and operating mostly from the more primitive parts of our brain.

There are, of course, any number of other ways that we might instinctively respond to Charlie, but given how draining life with a developmentally traumatized child is, in relation to the use of praise, the exhausted Hare may well find themselves trying the following ways of approaching Charlie's 'rude' behaviour.

Techniques
Without thinking too hard, we are likely to respond impulsively in the following ways:

- Trying to instil some common courtesy: shouting up the stairs after Charlie, 'I'd really rather you didn't speak to me like that!'
- Pride: 'Oh, well done, love! That's brilliant!' (shouted up the stairs after Charlie goes to her bedroom).

- Continued pride: (the next day as Charlie leaves for school) 'You did so well on that test, sweetheart'.

Traditional: praise (reward–punishment)
Approach

The traditional approach to this behaviour would have us focus on the behaviour alone. The behaviour to be encouraged may be Charlie's academic achievement. In this case, if her performance on the test was an achievement for her (it was better than might reasonably have been expected), then we might want to reward this with praise.

There are two alternatives to think about in this scenario. Paula and Dean may have decided that they really want to focus on helping Charlie do well academically. In this case they will praise her when she does well (by her own standards) so that she will be more likely to fulfil her academic potential.

Alternatively, Paula and Dean might see that 21 out of 40 is not as well as Charlie could have done and they believe that she didn't work as hard as she could have done for the test, so they would not praise her for this result (they will still be kind, of course – they are lovely people and they love Charlie). In this case, the absence of praise may raise some challenging feelings (and behaviours) for Charlie as she was so pleased about her result and the comments from her teacher.

If her carers did want to reinforce (reward) Charlie's achievement in the test, then they might employ the following praise-based techniques.

Techniques

- Charlie's success should be noticed and commented on specifically.
  - 'Wow, 21! That's more than last time!'
  - 'You got all of the capital cities?!'
  - 'You worked so hard on that test. Well done, Charlie!'
- Charlie would be praised in a way that she finds most

rewarding (however, due to the evaluative nature of these comments and how they conflict with her understanding of herself, she is unlikely to experience these comments as rewarding):

- 'You did brilliantly.'
- 'You superstar!'
- 'We're so proud of you.'

Therapeutic: celebration (EBM)
Approach

If we were to take a celebration-based approach to Charlie, we would focus first on her emotions, to work out what Charlie is feeling. As with many developmentally traumatized children, Charlie does not necessarily wear her real emotions clearly on her sleeve. They are masked by difficulties with trust and some defence against the frightening possibility that her fragile pride may be trampled on.

Seeing through Charlie's defences allows us to read her surliness and apparently casual attitude as happiness and most of all, pride. If Paula and Dean were taking this approach, they would focus on that and, because they are well attuned to Charlie, allow themselves to go with their own emotional experience of Charlie's feelings. They would then show Charlie how they are feeling verbally and non-verbally. Laying out in writing, as I'm doing here, an instinctive, emotional process makes it sound incredibly calculated, but this is far from how it would be in real life. Attunement to Charlie's emotions would mean that, when Paula and Dean have reminded themselves of the approach and given themselves permission to react emotionally, their connection would shine through without much thought required.

EBM also offers us the opportunity to acknowledge and talk about the 'surly attitude'. We address it rather than ignore it because it may cause Charlie problems in the future, and it may well damage the relationship between Charlie and her parent/carer. We might choose to address it on another day, or a different person in the family may bring it up. We would do this alongside celebration as a pure, factual, non-judgemental acknowledgment (see below).

Techniques

As with all the technique sections in this book there are many ways to apply the approach and you should adapt the ideas to suit your own voice and style.

- First, as described above, Paula and Dean would need to work out exactly how Charlie feels about her test results and the comments from her teacher. This is not always straightforward! They may try some emotional commentary to check out whether their hunches about how she feels are correct. This does not necessarily give the right answer, but it is possible to pick up clues. They may say,
  - 'Oh Charlie, you're so pleased.'
  - 'I wonder if, behind it all, you're really proud and excited about your result today?'
  - 'I know you don't like showing it, but I wonder if you feel good about what Mr Wright said?!'
  - 'I initially thought you were cross when you walked in! I reckon that was embarrassment or nervousness or something. Maybe you were worried we wouldn't get how well you've done.'
- If they conclude that Charlie is experiencing positive emotions, then, having tuned in to them, they would simply express their emotions honestly.
- The next step would be to assess, knowing Charlie, how well she takes to expressions of positive emotion. They would pitch their response in line with that, but they would err on the side of exuberance and help Charlie to handle it.
- It would be important for the celebration of Charlie's success to happen in person, face to face, and with time prioritized for it.
- They may express themselves in the following ways:
  - A hand-hold.
  - Wide eyes and a big smile.
  - A hug.
  - 'Oh Charlie! You did it!'

- 'I can't believe it, you worked so hard and you got such good comments!'
- Grabbing her for an excited hug and jumping up and down with her in their arms.

Hopefully it is clear in this example that the traditional praise-based techniques and the EBM celebration-based techniques would look very similar indeed. However, it should be equally clear that the approach that leads to the similar techniques is very different. This would lead the delivery and the relationship underneath the technique to feel very different for both parent and child.

Let's get practical
Working out what your child is feeling
Understanding 'why' (emotional commentary)

As discussed in the previous chapter, emotional commentary is a wonderful technique that covers a whole range of difficulties. It's so useful because showing your child that you understand their emotions and helping them to recognize them for themselves is a fundamental developmental process for traumatized children.

It can be used in two ways to help with celebration – first, in the way that Paula and Dean use it above, to test out with Charlie how she might be feeling. We cannot, when we use it this way, go looking for a definitive answer about how children are feeling; often our children cannot understand this themselves, let alone verbalize it. However, we can look for clues (body language, eye contact, what children say) as to whether what we tentatively suggest about feelings rings true with our child.

The second opportunity that emotional commentary offers is to connect emotionally with your child when you're celebrating with them. It helps children to feel heard and understood. It doesn't even matter whether or not you get their emotional state exactly right. The feeling that you want to understand their complicated emotional worlds with them is tremendously powerful. My toilet training metaphor can be useful in making sense of this. When we are helping a toddler understand when they need to use the toilet, we go through three steps:

1. We read the child's body language.
2. We commentate for them what they are experiencing: 'I think you need a wee' or 'You're doing the wee-wee dance'.
3. We act on our conclusion, that is, we take them to the toilet.

In doing this time and time again, children learn what their internal sensations mean and what to do about them. The same process is necessary for emotions. When children have missed out on the early experience in babyhood of someone noticing and acting on their emotions, they need it later in life. That is what emotional commentary does for children.

Examples of emotional commentary to help celebration include:

- 'Oh my goodness! Look at how happy you are!'
- 'Eek, you're so excited!'
- 'I can't work out whether you're unhappy or really proud.'
- 'Look at your smile! You are so pleased with what you've achieved!'

Emotional honesty

Once we've got a good guess about what a child is feeling and we've really taken that in, we can go with our own feelings (which are triggered via attunement to those of our child).

First, we need to check that our feelings and those of our child are consistent. Are we really feeling joyful with our child, or are we weighed down with the baggage of last night's argument or by the fact that they still haven't tidied their room after smashing it up last week? It's entirely possible that you might not feel fully attuned to your child's positive feelings for these or other reasons. To try and get back in tune, you might find some of the self-regulation strategies in Superpower #2: Safe Containment, or the grounding strategies in Superpower #1: Parental Self-Acceptance, helpful. If sharing joy, pride or excitement with your child is just not an honest place you can get yourself to, that's fine. Remember, self-acceptance and not self-discipline is the way through. Do whatever it is that works to get you restored and ready for next time. If emotional honesty in any given moment might result in criticism, judgement or annoyance, try something else until you're feeling more regulated.

If you can have a go at celebrating your child's positive feelings with them, then you might find yourself saying something along the lines of:

- 'It's so lovely you get to feel so happy about this!'
- 'I love it when things like this happen for you.'
- 'Eek! I'm so flipping proud of you!'
- 'Good for you, you did it!'
- 'I feel so happy and excited for you!'

The key way in which these are different to praise-based comments is that they focus on a shared emotion. We are not simply rewarding a child for doing what we wanted them to do regardless of the satisfaction they got from it.

Energy or vitality

Celebration requires a bit of an injection of energy. It may be that you see a very slight shadow of a good feeling in your child, but if it's rare, or your child doesn't often recognize or celebrate their success or happiness, you may decide to ramp it up a bit. The injection of your vitality will help to make this little good feeling into a big good feeling and be a much more pleasurable experience for both you and your child. Of course, you may need to moderate this a little if your child is unused to, or uncomfortable with, big emotional experiences. In this case start small and see if they can tolerate sharing a slightly bigger good feeling with you.

Non-verbal celebration

Some children and some celebrations may not lend themselves to being talked about; for example, if you're in a group of people and your child might feel too conspicuous or if it's a very subtle success or joy, then a conversation about it might feel too over the top. On these occasions, non-verbal celebration can work well. We also have to be mindful of how comfortable your child is with physical touch. This doesn't mean we never do it, but that we work towards a way that feels comfortable. Forgive me for labouring this point as it might seem obvious, but sometimes making the implicit explicit can really help parents to be aware of either what they are doing or what they might like to try doing differently.

Some examples of non-verbal celebration include:

- Eye contact.
- Big wide eyes and a smile.
- A wink.
- A gentle nudge.
- A stroke on the back.
- A hand squeeze.
- A hair ruffle.
- A thumbs up.
- Any secret sign that you make up between the two of you.

As well as sharing joy and success it can also be useful to share more challenging emotions. Our next chapter will take us through how we handle and share our children's difficult feelings.

SHARING DIFFICULT FEELINGS

Introduction

In this chapter we'll take a look at reassurance and its therapeutic alternative:

- 'Don't worry, I'll be back soon.'
- 'It'll be okay! Don't get upset. It doesn't matter that it's broken. We can get another one.'
- 'Oh, love, don't cry. It's not that bad!'

These are all fine examples of reassurance, of things we say when we are desperately trying to make a child feel better.

Reassurance is something along the lines of 'words of advice and comfort intended to make someone feel less worried or sad'. Despite this intention, reassurance is not very effective in making people feel less worried or sad. On the odd occasion that reassurance is actually reassuring, it depends on a few essential processes. It also requires that the person is not in a particularly heightened emotional state. Regulatory systems are not very effective when we are in the midst of a strong emotional reaction.

Examples of reassurance

Examples of reassurance include:

- 'There's no need to cry!'
- 'Take no notice.'
- 'You can do it!'
- 'They're only being mean because they're jealous.'
- 'Try not to worry.'
- 'It'll be okay.'
- 'It will be okay tomorrow.'
- 'You're not stupid/ugly/fat.'
- 'You have a lot to live for.'
- 'They don't mean it.'
- 'You're stronger than this.'
- 'It's not that bad!'
- 'You did your best.'
- 'Don't be upset.'
- 'They'll soon forget about it.'
- 'You're just tired.'
- 'You'll be fine.'
- 'You're alright.'
- 'Don't worry.'
- 'It doesn't matter.'

Typically, we reassure when someone is expressing difficult, often sad or worried, feelings. It's a great example of doing something through compassion but not necessarily with empathy. Reassurance comes when someone is feeling bad, and we don't want them to feel that way. However, it is also a product of not really wanting to 'go there' with them either.

When we are using reassurance, sometimes we are trying to make our child feel better, but if we're honest, sometimes we're trying to stop them passing us their negative or challenging feelings. It is sometimes a very real necessity for us to avoid big feelings, but it is a process that won't help our child. Please don't ever beat yourself up about that fact. It is *so* important to recognize and prioritize when we do need to do something for ourselves rather than for our child. Remember, both people in the therapeutic parenting relationship need to be looked after. On some occasions we have to be straight about the trade-off in that, and not everybody's needs can be met all the time. For a more thorough explanation of that idea, take a look at Superpower #1: Parental Self-Acceptance.

Reassurance in relation to reward–punishment thinking

Unlike many of our other 'parenting powers', reassurance isn't something that is prescribed as a 'technique' in traditional reward–punishment-based parenting. However, some types of reassurance are intrinsically reward–punishment-based, and are often a product of our Hare decision-making system.

Reassurance is something that happens in all relationships, especially emotionally charged ones, so we will address it and its alternatives in this chapter.

The message we send when we say 'Don't worry' is rarely effective in stopping a person worrying. It is either 'stop feeling that emotion' or 'stop expressing that emotion'. In this rather subtle way, reassurance has the effect of coaching people not to express their difficult emotions. It is an unconscious process (that we *all* take part in) driven by an impulse to avoid the feeling in question. We would often much rather emotions just go away.

Why do we reassure?

Unconsciously trying to make emotions just go away, via reassurance, is a very understandable drive. Sharing every single emotion of even a perfectly happy, healthy child is utterly exhausting. This is generally so much more exhausting with a child who has experienced early trauma. Just think about how many times a day there are grizzles, tantrums, upsets and fall-outs. Reassurance is a much quicker, easier option, and sometimes it doesn't do too much harm. However, we do need to think critically about how, when and why we use it.

Common companions of reassurance

It is the companions of reassurance, that is, the things we do alongside reassurance, that really make the difference as to whether reassurance can take on a therapeutic air or not. These companions change reassurance to be more suitable to different levels of emotional distress. The higher up the distress scale we go, the less significant and effective the reassurance itself is.

Reassuring words alone

This is often the domain of our Hare decision-making system. We all make these isolated, unemotional statements in response to the 1001 minor upsets in a day. What we say is 'It's okay, you can do it', 'It'll feel better in a few minutes'. What we typically mean is 'Please just get on with it without me for five minutes', 'Please just cope with it!'

Reassurance alone unconsciously communicates 'I can't really get into that right now', 'I don't want to deal with those feelings at the moment'. This isn't so harmful when emotional volume is low and with children who are reasonably able to regulate themselves. When this approach works, it would appear to be because it teaches children which low-level emotions can be safely ignored. This can be problematic for children who have a history of having their emotions ignored regardless of how big their feelings are. It serves to shut down conversation and connection rather than opening it up, which can be fine for some children in some circumstances, but may be problematic for others. Reassuring comments used in isolation, for children who are particularly sensitive and/or those who have experienced abuse, can be dismissive. For sensitive children, reassuring or dismissive responses may be hurtful and/or infuriating, and for traumatized children they may serve to reinforce their expectation that their feelings are inconsequential and that adults are dismissive and/or disconnected.

Motivational reassurance

This is when we reassure about difficult feelings and try to boost a child's confidence, often providing some sensory energy alongside; for example, 'I won't let you fall, don't worry! You can do it!'

We still lose that connecting sentiment with this kind of reassurance, so we might want to follow it up later with a discussion about what it was like to feel scared or worried. As ever, remember a key part of this approach is pragmatism. If you can see that this type of reassurance, or any other, works well for your child by helping them to feel more confident or allows them to express what's going on in their inner world, then go for it! Just bear in mind its potential pitfalls.

Reassurance with problem-solving

This technique could be summarized as something along the lines of 'It'll be okay. Let's work out what's going on and see if we can sort it out.'

This can work well with children who do okay with a rational, cognitive approach and who aren't hugely distressed. It's a connected and collaborative approach and offers a child the sense that they don't have to shoulder their worry alone. However, it is purely cognitive (thought-based) and therefore not connecting with a child on an emotional level (feeling-based). This can be problematic for children whose level of distress is high or their ability to regulate their feelings is poor.

Reassurance with empathy

This approach can be exemplified as 'Oh honey, you're really upset about this! It's going to be okay', combined with a compassionate tone and a tight hug. The reassurance statement is the short part at the end, 'It's going to be okay', and it is laden with empathy and emotional connection. This technique is the most demanding of time and energy but it is likely to be the most effective type of reassurance for children who have experienced trauma. It conveys an emotional, sensory *and* verbal message of reassurance. It incorporates containment (feeding back the child's emotions safely and calmly) and **intersubjectivity** (the empathic communication of emotions consciously and unconsciously). It invites connection and to some degree opens up the potential for conversation about what the child is experiencing.

Later in this chapter we will move on to thinking about a similar technique, but one that takes out the reassuring statements altogether. It is also useful, however, to take things in the opposite direction and consider where reassurance without empathy and connection can lead us.

Beyond reassurance...

At its worst, reassurance can encourage us to see children's distress signals as 'naughtiness' or 'playing up'. Some reassurance can be about talking children out of what they are feeling. 'Don't worry/Don't cry/It's okay', said with a short temper and irritation, can feel like 'What you are feeling is wrong and you just need to stop feeling it'. Remember, there is no judgement here. We *all* do this sometimes. Reacting this way is of more benefit to us than it is to our children. We are asking children to 'just deal with it' or 'just ignore it' when the majority of developmentally traumatized children have much less of an idea of how to deal with emotions than other children.

Let's be clear, though, it's a sad fact that there are times when we have no energy to deal with a child's emotional world. This is sad, yes, but not deserving of judgement. By unpacking what is going on when we reassure, we can really drill down into, and reflect on, the difference between using reassurance because we simply have nothing left, and using reassurance because we think it's the best thing to do. When we're in those exhausted states or we're emotionally frazzled ourselves, and our Hare system takes over, we can stumble down slippery slopes to really unhelpful places beyond reassurance. When confronted with an emotional experience of one of our children, there isn't one of us who hasn't said, or been tempted to say, something along the lines of 'Stop being so silly!' or 'Be quiet now or there'll be no playtime'. In doing this, we succeed only in dismissing and punishing our children for expressing their feelings to us.

As we've discussed, there are times when we cannot be empathic in the face of emotional expression, and there are children for whom emotional need feels like a bottomless pit. In the section below we will talk about techniques we can use when we feel like we can't handle our children's emotion and might be drawn towards unhelpful reassurance or dismissing or punishing our children's emotions.

What do we mean by sharing difficult feelings?

So what is the alternative to reassurance when we're faced with the sadness, anger or worry of our child?

The attractive thing about reassurance, and the reason we

probably gravitate to it so readily, is because it is quick and requires very little of us, physically, mentally or emotionally, and sometimes it maybe even appears to work!

In these moments of distress, worry, sadness or anger, we can try another way. Rather than trying to close down the conversation by convincing our children that they simply shouldn't have the emotional reaction they're having, we can try sharing the load with them. We can try carrying a couple of those emotional bags for our child. Rather than trying to make the feeling go away, we can accept its existence and try to connect with it via empathy. This enables children to offload some of the burden of that feeling. It also enables us to regulate their feelings with them – as we know, emotional regulation is one of the things that developmentally traumatized children struggle with most. Co-regulation not only eases the burden for your child in the moment, but it also helps to internalize the regulation process so that they are more likely to be able to cope with emotional reactions independently in the future.

There can be some (understandable) reluctance to opening up emotions rather than keeping them locked down. Sometimes when we start using this technique, it can feel like we're making feelings bigger, not smaller. In many cases this is exactly what will happen because we're telling our children that we will listen more and more attentively to what is going on in their inner worlds, so, of course, they are more likely to share more of it. This can feel overwhelming to begin with, but it is reassuring to know that we are not making it worse; we are connecting with the worst of what our child has bubbling away within themselves.

What can I do when I've got nothing left?

The alternative to reassurance, the thing that enables greater connection between children and their parents and carers, is far more effortful and demanding of adults. Sharing challenging emotions requires the adults involved to be very well attuned to their own emotional state and to be careful about what resources they have available at any given time.

There are times, based on careful self-reflection, when parents will have to assert to themselves that they *do not* have the emotional resources to co-regulate their child's emotions. At these times, rather than reassurance, I would urge you to confront the truth of the dilemma with your child. Rather than slipping back to 'It's okay, don't worry', it's more connecting and regulatory to say something akin to 'I know you're feeling bad at the moment, I'm so sorry, I'm feeling so tired that I can't really chat about it now. Could we have a chat about it later?' or 'I get that you're worried and I really want to understand, but we just need to just get home right now. Can we chat in an hour when we're home and everyone else is sorted with something to do?'

Now we'll think through the process when a child is expressing a difficult emotion and they're asking (verbally or non-verbally) for support. To clarify exactly how traditional and therapeutic approaches and techniques may be similar or different, we will look at what might be a textbook response to a real-life scenario. This will help us to explore what therapeutic parenting (specifically EBM) is all about (and crucially, what it isn't). As well as looking at what each of the approaches would have us aspire to, we will also explore a more real-life example of how our exhausted Hare might react.

✴ AHMED AND ZAINAB

Ahmed is a 6-year-old boy living with his grandma, Zainab, under a Special Guardianship Order. He, his grandma and his 5-year-old sister are out at their local play park. They've had a good day; they've been grocery shopping and things have been fairly harmonious. Ahmed has been on the see-saw with his sister and played on the swings. He tells his grandma that he's bored of them and wants to go on the climbing frame, but he's scared he will fall.

Reality: the exhausted Hare	Traditional: reassurance	Therapeutic: sharing difficult feelings
✗	✗	✓
(Unpredictable)	(Not trauma-informed)	(Trauma-informed)

Comparison of approaches

Reality: the exhausted Hare
Approach

Before we start to think about what traditional and then EBM approaches would encourage us to do in response to Ahmed, we need to do a check-in with our poor exhausted Hare, Zainab. Remember, this relates back to the Hare decision-making system, the impulsive, quick way we generally make decisions, particularly when we are stressed and operating mostly from the more primitive parts of our brain.

Specifically, in relation to the pull towards reassurance, the exhausted Hare may well deal with Ahmed in the following ways. There are, of course, any number of other ways that we might instinctively respond, but given what a challenge life with a developmentally traumatized child can be, this is one realistic example.

Techniques

Without thinking too hard, we are likely to respond impulsively in the following ways:

- 'Oh come on, Ahmed. You can do it, you're a big boy now.'
- 'Don't be silly, you'll be fine.'
- 'Look, even your little sister is doing it!'

Traditional: reassurance (reward–punishment)
Approach

The traditional approach to this behaviour would be to focus on the behaviour alone. Although it may not appear so at first glance, reassurance is fundamentally reward–punishment-based. When we approve of the boy who hides his tears or the girl who takes her worries to the bedroom, we are rewarding the repression of emotion.

Reassurance, in this case, is trying to train Ahmed out of feeling worried. The techniques used may be very similar to those listed above that could well be used when our Hare decision-making system comes into play.

Techniques

If Ahmed's grandma was trying to shape his behaviour by using reward–punishment-based techniques (including unconsciously trying to train him out of worrying), she might try something along these lines:

- 'You can do it!'
- 'Brilliant! You got yourself to the bottom, now see if you can try one little step! Fantastic!'
- 'You're fine. If you manage to get to the top, you can have a treat when we get home.'
- 'No, you're fine. I'm not going to help you, you can do it.'

Therapeutic: sharing difficult feelings (EBM)

Approach

First, we would approach Ahmed's worry about the climbing frame, as we always would when using EBM, from the position of emotions first. We need to work out what Ahmed might be feeling and why. We work hard to get inside his head and understand what it feels like to be Ahmed in that moment. This sounds long and involved, but in practice it is the work of seconds.

Techniques

- If Zainab was to try an EBM approach, she would first check in on how *she* was feeling to see whether she had enough emotional energy to be authentically empathic to Ahmed and his feelings about the climbing frame.
- Her task is to share his feelings and to try and regulate them for him so that he can achieve what he wants to achieve (not necessarily what she thinks he should want to achieve).
- To do this she needs to accept his feelings (avoiding the temptation to change them!) and she might then try to commentate on what she thinks and feels that Ahmed is feeling. For example:

- 'You're feeling scared aren't you, darling? It's so difficult to do scary things!'
- 'It's so confusing for you! I can see how much you want to climb up, but it's scary too!'
- 'You really want to try something new, but it's making you feel worried too! Can I help you just a little bit?'

Let's get practical
Empathic commentary
Examples of empathic commentary in regard to co-regulation or sharing difficult feelings are:

- 'Oh, you're so worried about your friend being mean to you today.'
- 'Sweetheart, you look so sad today.'
- 'You seem angry because your brother turned the TV over. I understand. I'm sorry, honey. Let's sort it out if we can.'
- 'No wonder you're frustrated! I just said you can't go out with your friends and you really, really want to! I'm so sorry!' (This doesn't mean your decision necessarily changes.)

Reassurance vs. empathic commentary to share difficult feelings

Reassurance	Sharing difficult feelings
'There's no need to cry!'	'You're feeling so sad!'
'They don't mean it.'	'You're really feeling bad about what they said.'
'It's not that bad!'	'You're feeling awful, aren't you?'
'You did your best.'	'You seem worried about how that went.'
'You're just tired.'	'You're finding things overwhelming right now, aren't you?'
'You'll be fine.'	'You're so worried/sad. I'm so sorry.'
'Don't worry.'	'You're feeling really worried about this.'
'It doesn't matter.'	'This feels so important!'

Emotional honesty

For those times when reassurance takes a dismissive tone (we've all been there) – for example, 'Come on, it doesn't matter', 'Stop crying now, it's not that bad' – empathy and understanding just aren't available to us. There are, however, better alternatives than dismissive 'reassurance'.

Emotional honesty in relation to reassurance requires us to be aware of our own reactions to the emotional demands that children place on us. This is a discipline in itself and is required for all therapeutic and empathic parenting, and it takes practice! Our goal is to see that how we feel and the way we want to impulsively react to our child is down to a combination of their 'stuff' and ours. What they say, do and feel is communicated to us, and we process it based on how we feel and what our previous experiences are. We can often convince ourselves that our reactions are objective and just and directly caused by what our child has done or said, but it's really not as simple as that.

If we can observe the emotions in our reactions to our children, we can take a breath and give a reasonably safe, contained and emotionally honest response. This would look something like the following:

- 'Oh, love, I'm so sorry we can't chat about it now. Can we talk later?'
- 'Sweetheart, I'm feeling really quite stressed at the minute because I'm trying to carry all the shopping and get in the house. Give me 20 minutes and we'll have a chat. I'm sorry I can't do it right now.'
- 'I get that you're cross with your brother. I'm feeling a bit wound up about it myself at the moment. We'll both be fine in a bit. Just go into the other room for a few minutes to keep away from him, then I'll come and chat in a minute.'
- 'I know you want a cuddle. I definitely want to make you feel better, but blimey it's been a tricky morning! I feel like I need to sort myself out for five minutes, then I'll be right with you.'

Making sure we have the time and space to regulate ourselves when we're surrounded by emotional need can enable us to respond more sensitively in the end. This is not a way of disciplining children to wait and it is not really about teaching them anything. It is about us and our ability to do what needs to be done in as empathic a way as possible.

Listening with wonder

One of the most profound disadvantages of reassurance is that it invites us to talk more than listen. The talking comes from a good place, a desire to make the worry or sadness, etc. go away – to talk it into non-existence. We can buck this temptation by simply not talking when faced with big feelings that might invite us to reassure. Listen more. If we take this time, then when we do talk, we can talk with the purpose of facilitating our children to talk. For example, you could try the following:

- 'You look worried, honey...'
- 'You feel a bit scared of the spider, hey?'
- 'Oh, you really don't want to go to school! I wonder why?'
- 'Wow! You sound so cross...'

Non-verbal co-regulation

As well as all of the verbal strategies that we can try, non-verbal regulation of emotion is essential. This can be alongside verbal techniques or it can stand alone. Non-verbal techniques can take any number of forms. Once you get the hang of it, you'll be able to work out what works best for your child. The important thing is to give yourself the time to focus and engage with what is going on for your child, to find your empathy. If you can feel what your child is feeling and show it, you'll already be starting to regulate them. Here are a few ideas about showing this non-verbally. Children have different levels of tolerance for physical contact, so take your time and work out what works for them at different times.

- Sitting down by your child's side.
- Eye contact, mirroring their expression (if your child can tolerate this – not all children can).

- An expression that says 'I feel your pain'.
- A hand-hold/squeeze.
- Strokes on the back.
- A big hug.
- A one-armed squeeze.

Empathic encouragement or motivation

Sometimes we can be invited to reassure children when they are having difficult feelings about trying something new or tricky. Our first port of call to be more empathic is to deploy our empathic strategies (see above) to help co-regulate the tricky emotions. We can then think about how to physically and sensorially create an atmosphere of confidence for our children. The essence of this is: 'I know you have big feelings about this. I think I can help you do it even with those feelings.' We can do this by conveying our understanding of their worries but also their abilities. This is often about creating optimistic energy through playful exuberance. Below are some ideas about how this might be done; as always, once you've got the idea behind it, you'll come up with ways that suit you and your child.

- 'It's scary to think about going up the climbing frame, isn't it? I know! Follow me! I hope it can take my weight!' (Parent gives some 'eeks' and squeals as they go up too.)
- 'I hear how cross you are with Dad. Should we see if we can sneak up to the door to see him? [Whispers] Don't let him spot you!! Aaargh! He saw us! Run away!'
- 'You're worried about me going to work and leaving you at Grandma's aren't you? [Leaving time to talk, if that feels like it would help, a big hug and a conversation about when you'll be back, transitional object (that is, an object associated with safety that can be safely taken with the child, such as a much loved teddy or a photograph of the child with their family), etc.] I know those feelings might not have gone but, okay, we're gonna do it. 1-2-3 let's go!'

When sharing the messy inner world of our children (or even narrating on the fact that we can't at times), we are being thoughtful and responsive to our needs and those of our children. In the next chapter we'll go on to talk about responsiveness and its traditional cousin, 'consistency'.

RESPONSIVENESS

Introduction

When using reward–punishment logic we are told to be consistent in our responses to behaviour, regardless of its causes and the emotional state of our child. Whilst stability and predictability are incredibly therapeutic, these things do not need to be rigidly (or necessarily consistently) applied at the cost of responsiveness to our children's emotional needs.

When we're talking about boundary setting, rewards and consequences, consistency and clarity become very important indeed. Consistency really does have the potential to bring about predictability and a sense for children that the world is knowable. We all know how incredibly important a sense of safety is for developmentally traumatized children. In this way, consistency, with regard to rules and boundaries, is important. However, the downside of consistent application of rewards and punishments is that it requires us to ignore the reason behind any breaking of the rules. It invites us to ignore our children's inner worlds. We are left with only reactions to what they do, not what they think or feel. As we've discussed in previous chapters, this is hugely problematic given what we know about how much our children have to deal with their inner worlds. We know that early trauma can fundamentally change how people see the world, how they approach it, how they feel about it and how *any* interactions are perceived. It is clear that the tussle between consistency and responsiveness is no simple issue for us in our therapeutic parenting. Let's pick apart what it all means in detail.

Consistency in reward–punishment thinking

Consistency is one of the key tenets of making reward–punishment strategies work. When we set a rule, we need to stick to it, right? If we enforce it on one day and then don't the next (for example, we give a reward for doing the washing-up on one occasion and then not the next), we are sending mixed messages. Reward–punishment logic tells us that we are confusing our children, and our efforts to guide them to follow a certain way of being will be ineffective.

For any of us, clarity – knowing what is expected and what consequences for rule breaks will be – is important. If, for example, we're driving around a quiet car park, in a hurry to get out, we will easily be drawn into driving against the arrow flow if we can clearly see that the 20-metre road is clear. If, on the other hand, we see cars coming down, perhaps it's a busier day, or we see a traffic warden or a police car, we will avoid breaking the rules.

Quite apart from its influence on whether people stick to the rules, consistency also has an important role to play in therapeutic parenting. Consistency can help us to understand our environment; it makes the world feel reliable, predictable and safe. However, consistency is at its most therapeutic when it is supportive and containing, and not when it is rigid. When it is used flexibly, sensitively and in a way that is responsive to the circumstances and emotional imperatives, it is at its most powerful. Imagine, for example, driving around that same car park and swerving down a road the opposite way to the signs in order to avoid an accident. You would feel aggrieved to get a fine or even a telling-off for doing so under these circumstances. However, that is what unswerving consistency is. It is prioritizing, not confusing people about a rule, over understanding why they might have broken that rule.

It is not always the case, but consistency can invite us to take an approach of stern rigidity. We can easily get into the mentality that being a good parent means 'not giving in' and 'not backing down'. Acknowledging how important something is to your child before you enforce a 'boundary' can be hard (particularly if you're as stubborn as I am). However, it doesn't need to feel like admitting defeat; you can make that reassessment an active, assertive choice.

What do we mean by responsiveness?

In many ways, responsiveness is the exact opposite of consistency. Responsiveness means putting an understanding of why a person can be moved to break the rules over the strict enforcement of those rules.

As parents and carers, we often instinctively apply responsiveness in relation to rules and boundaries, but the degree to which we do this varies a huge amount between us. We respond sensitively to our children and their indiscretions, particularly the smaller ones. We think about why children have broken rules. However, reward–punishment thinking encourages us to be more consistent and less responsive to the emotional causes. It invites us to switch off our sensitivity to emotional drives.

As well as responsiveness in relation to rule breaks, we also need to think about consistency and responsiveness in relation to boundary setting. For example, imagine your child walking in from school having had a fall-out with their best friend. They tell you the ins and outs of it and they are still subdued and quiet and look close to tears. They are struggling to find the motivation to do anything productive or fun, and only want a quick hug. You know that they have already reached the limit of their screen time for the day, but you also know that when they play games on their tablet, they feel relaxed and content. In these circumstances, the responsive thing to do is indulge that emotional need for contentment and soothing and celebrate your ability to comfort your child in the only way they can accept in that moment. It would be sensible to create a narrative around this for your child of describing how upset they seem and how nothing else you want to offer them seems to feel like it's making it feel any better for them. The extra screen time can be described as a rare luxury, because 'I want you to feel better but rules around how much we use the tablet are still really important'. You could then explain that it will only be until teatime and hopefully that will help things feel better. On the other hand, the consistent thing to do is to continue to stick to the rule about screen time and allow your child to go without the comfort that you know it would bring.

Like many parenting decisions, there is a balancing act to be done with consistency and responsivity. Balancing the priorities of helping your child to feel safe and secure within a predictable environment (that comes from consistency) and prioritizing their need for comfort and emotional understanding (via responsiveness) is tough, and a stern and rigid approach to either risks missing important emotional needs. When we slip too far towards rigid consistency, we risk missing opportunities to acknowledge and regulate challenging emotions. Erring too far towards responsiveness may lead to confusion and a reduction in felt safety (emotional and physical).

Now we'll think through the process, when the need for decisions about consistency vs. responsivity arises, in relation to a particular event. To clarify exactly how the traditional and therapeutic (EBM) approaches and techniques may be similar or different, we will explore what might be a textbook response to a real-life scenario. This will help us to explore what EBM is all about (and what it isn't). As well as looking at what each of the approaches would have us aspire to, we will also explore a more real-life example of how our exhausted Hare might react.

✸ THE WRIGHT FAMILY

The Wright family have a rule about not shouting at each other. It's really important for foster carers Janette and Michael that their foster children don't shout at them or at each other. Their youngest foster child, Kayden, gets very frightened by raised voices. Jermaine (8 years old) struggles with this; he seems to just have a loud voice even when he's relatively calm. One afternoon, from downstairs, Michael hears Jermaine, who is upstairs, shouting very loudly at his sister Yasmin.

It wasn't clear at the time but Jermaine was shouting at Yasmin because she was opening the latch of her bedroom window to look out. Jermaine knows this is dangerous and he is, in his way, trying to prevent her falling by shouting at her. The children have experienced neglect and Jermaine was held responsible by his birth parents for the behaviour of his younger siblings.

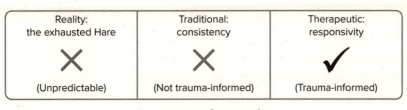

Reality: the exhausted Hare	Traditional: consistency	Therapeutic: responsivity
✗	✗	✓
(Unpredictable)	(Not trauma-informed)	(Trauma-informed)

Comparison of approaches

Reality: the exhausted Hare
Approach
Before we start to think about what traditional and then EBM approaches would encourage us to do in response to Jermaine, it's useful to think about what our instinctive, impulsive Hare system decision-making might lead us to do.

In the moment, it is very likely that we will have an angry or irritated reaction. Michael, in our example, is dealing with three young children; he's just back from the school run and he and Janette have spoken to Jermaine many, many times about shouting. They've tried being strict and stern, and they've talked to him calmly and explained why it's so important, but still it keeps happening.

In this frame of mind, Michael goes up the stairs and shouts, 'What is going on Jermaine?! Why are you shouting at your sister?! I've told you a hundred times, shouting is not acceptable in this house!' Jermaine reacts by getting angry in return and shouts at Michael to 'Shut up!' The whole situation descends pretty quickly into a huge fall-out, from which the bad feeling lasts for days.

Techniques
The 'techniques', if we can even call them that, might be something along the lines of:

- Intervening immediately to make the shouting stop.
- Physically intervening, moving Jermaine away from his sister.
- Shouting at Jermaine (about the fact he shouldn't be shouting...).
- Angrily sending Jermaine to his room (for time out).

Traditional: consistency (reward–punishment)

Approach

From this approach we view the priority as deterring Jermaine from shouting at his sister again. The textbook approach might be to discourage parents and carers from acting emotionally and to apply the consequence that had previously been agreed on.

Techniques

- Engaging in minimal conversation with Jermaine.
- Approaching Jermaine calmly and assertively.
- Paying minimal attention to Jermaine's protestations about why he behaved the way he did or his angry reaction to the consequence.
- Applying consequences such as:
  - Sending Jermaine to his room for up to eight minutes (a minute for each year).
  - Telling Jermaine that he had lost his screen time for that evening.
  - Stopping Jermaine from going swimming the next day.

Therapeutic: responsivity (EBM)

Approach

This approach would still encourage Michael to hold in mind the children's need for predictability and safety (via consistently responding to a problem behaviour) but alongside understanding Jermaine's motivation for shouting.

Techniques

- Self-acceptance for Michael, accepting that he's frustrated and angry and may not be capable of his best parenting in the moment.
- Michael finding some way to cope in the moment and coming back to the issue later (striking whilst the iron is cold).

Alternatively, accepting he responded as our exhausted Hare did, but repairing and being responsive later.

- There could be a puzzled, curious approach to Jermaine: 'Hmmm, I wonder why you shouted at Yasmin even though you know it's a really bad idea.'
- Michael could try a gentle, nurturing touch that Jermaine feels comfortable with.
- The situation could be defused with silliness (but NOT sarcasm): 'Oh my goodness, did I leave the TV on up here? I heard someone shouting and I know it couldn't be you two!'
- Michael could try showing an understanding of why: 'Aha, you were shouting to keep Yasmin safe! Thank you, mate, that was such a kind thing to try and do!'
- There may be a way of addressing the problematic behaviour in an accepting way: 'You shouted because you thought it would help! Shouting makes Kayden scared though, doesn't it? I don't want you to shout but I get why you did. Is there any other way you could carry on keeping your brother and sister safe without shouting?'
- Michael could focus on taking away the shame and giving hope: 'Proud of you, mate. We'll get there and crack the shouting thing soon enough.'

Let's get practical

You might also find the techniques listed in Superpower #2: Safe Containment useful in relation to consistency and responsiveness.

Understanding yourself

The place to start when we're thinking about consistency vs. responsiveness is with you. Ask yourself some key questions.

Question one: What was your childhood experience of consistency, boundaries, rule setting and responsiveness?

This is a big topic that can apply to each and every dilemma we come up against in therapeutic parenting. Getting to grips with this is a life's work, but each little area we reflect on helps to reduce our unconscious, defensive responses to our children. It enables us to respond authentically to the child in front of us and not to our own past. To explore this further you might like to take a look at the work of Dan Siegel[45] or Kim Golding.[46]

Many of us grew up at a time when adherence to the say-so of an authority figure was absolute. If you didn't, there would be physical punishment to deal with along with its consequent fury, resentment, despair and rebellion. We may have experienced frustrated rage at not being heard when we had a good reason for doing something, even though it broke the rules. You may have had an experience of very little containment and nobody really taking care of making life predictable or feeling safe.

We need to think carefully about what effect these experiences have on our parenting. Are we tempted to over-compensate in the other direction, or in the heat of the moment can we find ourselves re-enacting the parenting we experienced? Alternatively, perhaps because your early experience was unproblematic, it's hard to motivate yourself to do anything differently: 'It didn't do me any harm!'

Question two: How do you feel in the heat of the moment when you're trying to assert a rule?

One thing we need to be very eagle-eyed for is the feelings that you experience when your child resists your attempts to consistently apply a rule. When you're running this through, think about where you are taken in terms of both force and strength (see Superpower #1: Parental Self-Acceptance). For many of us, one or more things can happen:

- We get ourselves trapped into a stubbornness cycle where neither of us is willing to give up, and so the interaction becomes less connected and more punitive. This can very easily lead to...
- A rageful feeling that forces us to make sure we 'win' by any means necessary. This can become dangerous. Mostly we are bigger and stronger than our children and we are capable of overpowering them with physical force.

- We unassertively give up and retain our sense of failure and resentment. In this and the previous scenario we have set up a win–lose power dynamic, and neither 'winning' nor 'losing' is good for us, or for our children. Remember, as discussed above, calmly and assertively deciding not to battle with our children and dealing with the issue at another time, in another way, is different to this, and can demonstrate great strength to our children.

Regulating yourself

Finding a way to stay emotionally regulated and calm is our biggest asset in these interactions, and shows strength without force. Our (sometimes incredibly difficult) job on these occasions is to stay calmer and more in control of ourselves than our children are able to. If we dysregulate as much as them, interactions go nowhere good at all. For more detail on self-regulation, take a look at Superpower #1: Parental Self-Acceptance.

Being in control for (not of) your child

I just can't bring myself to call this section 'boundaries'. It's a perfectly good word for what I'm trying to describe, but it conjures up all the opposite feelings, and makes us approach the topic in traditional ways. The language of 'boundaries' directs us to think in a reward–punishment way and to a non-therapeutic mindset, one that frames parenting in terms of discipline, consequences and 'good' behaviour.

We talked in Superpower #2: Safe Containment about being in control *for* rather than being in control *of* our children. This is a useful way to refocus us on the evidence of what our children need and what works. It offers an alternative to the invitations to do what we've always done, what other people expect us to do, or what is instinctive as a result of our own parenting experiences.

The issue of parental control is key to the discussion of consistency vs. responsiveness but it would more easily be associated with the former than the latter. If we are consistent in imposing rules, then we are most obviously asserting our control (most often for our children's benefit, but sometimes for other reasons). However, we can choose to be proactive and think about responsiveness as creating control and safety for our children too (such as assertively changing our mind). We must always remind ourselves not to confuse force with strength. Consistency requires us to use force; responsiveness requires us to show strength.

Okay, so how do we do it? How do we establish control on behalf of our children in a therapeutic way? Remember, moving a notch or two towards responsiveness and away from rigid consistency is not a move towards permissiveness. Children need their adults to lead them, to show them the way, and to help them to navigate. The following are just a few pointers to which you can add your own when you get the hang of it.

Developing the 'being in control for' mindset

Think of yourself as a leader (or co-leader) of your family. You're not the only one with answers and you will get things wrong. You have the responsibility for guiding how the family and its individual members do things, but you're not the only one who has a say. You're willing to admit when your idea about how to do things isn't as good as you first thought or someone else has a better one.

You're the one who has to make sure things get done and everyone is safe. You have responsibility for helping your children to achieve their potential as best you can and understanding what they need to be happy. Sometimes your role as leader will mean people get annoyed or upset with you. You can listen to those feelings and take them in without necessarily taking them as a personal criticism.

- When things your child has done aren't okay, you can say they are not okay, but do it in the following ways:
    - Connect with your child emotionally.
    - Be straightforward.
    - Be calm.
    - Be loving.
    - Be assertive.
    - Don't use shame.

- Understand why they did it or how they got to a place where doing what they did made sense.

• Try to hold in mind your whole child, not just the bit that has done something you don't like.

• Explain why what they have done isn't okay. Sometimes this will need to be a good while after the event if your child is distressed or dysregulated. Say it lovingly and minimize shame.

• Don't pretend like nothing bad has happened, but choose your moment to bring it up. The best time would be when you and your child are calm, and they are feeling loved.

• Commentate kindly on your own feelings if you're struggling to regulate yourself.

• Remember that changing a rule in response to your child's reaction to it isn't necessarily giving in. Whilst we need to test children's tolerance and motivate them to do more of what is good for them and for others, pushing them beyond their 'window of tolerance' won't help anyone (see Superpower #9: Building Motivation and Hope).

• Decide to change your mind (assertively). If, having tried for three sessions to get your child to Brownies, you are still faced with screaming, crying, distress, change the rule! You have not given in; you have responded to your child's distress, and they have shown you that it's more difficult than perhaps either of you thought it would be. You've tried, but now is not a good time for Brownies. Don't persist on a point of principle. Say to yourself, your child and Brown Owl: 'We thought it was a good idea but actually it's not right now. We might try again another time.'

• Decide *not* to change your mind (with empathy). When your application of the rules upsets your child, you can express your sorrow, you can say sorry! It doesn't necessarily mean that you think changing the rule is the right thing to do.

You can hold their hand and help them deal with the feelings that the rule and your assertion of it have caused.

Empathic commentary

Empathic commentary can help enormously when we're trying to talk ourselves around to being responsive rather than rigidly consistent. It gets us into an empathic frame of mind. Examples include:

- 'It's so hard for you when I point out that you need to tidy your room. I'm sorry it makes you so cross.'
- 'Okay, I see that you're struggling to hold things together now and talking to me isn't helping. Would a bit of telly time help? I know it's more than we've agreed for today, but I can see how nothing else is helping. It'll be back to the normal rules tomorrow.'
- 'Right, we've tried with you brushing your teeth by yourself for a few days now, but it still seems as difficult as it was when we started! I think you're not ready yet. Let's go back to me doing it for you and we'll try again in a few months' time. I'm sorry this got so stressful for you.'
- 'It's feeling extra hard today to hear that we're going to stick with just one hour of telly time today, I guess because you really needed extra time yesterday. I'm afraid I really don't think you need extra today. I'm sorry.'

One of the key changes in mindset we need, when adjusting to responsiveness over consistency, is developing an ability to get inside our child's inner world and to begin to explore 'why'. In the next chapter we will pick apart the invitation to find out the facts when something goes wrong as opposed to understanding the emotional context (the 'why') of that scenario.

EXPLORING 'WHY?'

Introduction

As a parent or carer, there is a startling amount of information coming your way at any given moment. A crying 6-year-old, a silent and sullen 15-year-old, a complaining and annoyed 10-year-old are all (sometimes simultaneously) sending you messages to deal with. The sensory impact of all that on us is quite something and we are obliged to impose some order on it all. What do we do with all that information, and how do we deal with everything that each of our children throws our way?

Well, the default answer is that we often seek to evaluate it in a multitude of ways. Whose fault is it? How annoying is it to us? Do we think it's justified? Is it an appropriate reaction? Does it require us to act on it? Whilst we are asking these questions, excavating the 'truth' about what has happened and working out who did what to whom, we can miss what is often the most obvious and crucial information we are given: what is being expressed? What is my child going through right now? Rarely do we take the time to pause and accept our child's reaction just as it is and invest in understanding it and what it feels like to be them in that moment. It is in this spirit that we ask the therapeutic question 'why?' It is not to interrogate or even to seek factual information; rather, it engages us curiously with the inner worlds of our children. For further information about curiosity in this context, you may find Dan Hughes'[47, 48] and Kim Golding's[49] work useful.

Evaluation in reward–punishment thinking

Evaluation starts with the preconception that we need to evaluate what has happened and decide what we need to do. It comes from the feeling of a need to act, to *do* something. When we investigate the 'truth' of a situation in order to decide whether we should do something, we are behaving in line with reward–punishment thinking. We are judging what has happened and considering whether to apply a consequence, either good or bad.

Focus on behaviour

One of the challenging elements of evaluation is that it compels us to focus on behaviour, to think only about what is done rather than what is felt. When we react to the behaviour of our children with an expectation of having to *do* something, rather than to simply understand and contain, we bypass two major parts of the puzzle: first, the chance to connect with our children in a way that promotes acceptance and undermines shame; and second, focusing on behaviour can prevent us from getting to an emotional understanding that may well cause troublesome behaviour to go away. After all, when we undercut shame and help children to regulate, we increase a child's opportunity to engage positively in their relationship with us and with the world around them. By looking predominantly at behaviour, we effectively hobble ourselves. Why do we do this? Because it's what everybody does! It's the way people generally react to us, so it becomes instinctive. We also tend to focus more on policing than nursing because it is so much less emotionally demanding and effortful. Engaging with someone who is being difficult and emotional is hard!

The inner police officer

Our compulsion to evaluate, and thus to focus on behaviour, sets us up as a necessarily punitive figure. We become, if you like, the police officer of this scenario (apologies to police officers reading this, I know I'm massively over-simplifying here). We become an authority figure, about whom our child has to be wary. Abuse and/or neglect prime many of our children to anticipate unfairness, and to feel that trust is a bad idea. In our police officer role, we are positioned as the person who will find out what has happened, who is to blame and who should be punished. However, there is another role that may help everyone involved to tell the truth and get what they need from the situation, not just the 'victim' (see below for further discussion of the alternative 'inner negotiator' role).

When developmentally traumatized children are fearful of being punished, they often bring an expectation that they may be unfairly punished or given responsibility for something over which they have little power. This expectation will trigger the parts of the brain that deal with fear. It is therefore more likely, in these situations, that our children will make reactive Hare system decisions rather than rational Tortoise system decisions. In these situations we are likely to be more suspicious – 'He's trying to trick me', 'Watch out for the trap' – and/or defensive – 'You're always having a go at me!', 'I didn't do anything!', 'It was her!' When we are suspicious and defensive, we do not cooperate, and we are not focused on understanding or solving problems. This applies to all of us. Just think of a time you've felt this way, when you've felt under scrutiny or even attack, like someone is trying find something out about you that they will judge you negatively for. Just how collaborative did you feel?

What do we mean by exploring 'why?'?

Settling in and exploring 'why?' rather than getting your private investigator's magnifying glass out to look at 'what?' sounds deceptively simple, but it's not intuitive. In order to get into the habit of doing it, it's worth bearing in mind the following ideas. These are taken from their definition in the therapeutic literature, particularly from the work of Dan Hughes[50, 51] and Kim Golding[52, 53] and their work on Dyadic Developmental Psychotherapy (DDP) (a therapy based on the potential of healthy, therapeutic parenting relationships to heal relational trauma).

Acceptance

True acceptance is actually quite a big leap from how we typically do things. When we encounter some problematic behaviour or state of mind in our children, we begin with the powerful, overarching mindset that 'This needs to change' or 'It's my responsibility to make this change'. Truly embracing acceptance means doing our best to back away from that impulse. It means stepping back and abandoning thoughts of change (perhaps only temporarily) to stay in the moment and accept the emotional status quo.

Acceptance means that right here and right now, this thing is the way it is: 'My child is angry' – fact. 'My child is angry enough to have hit someone' – fact. 'My child feels the need to lie to me' – fact. 'My child feels that I'm being unfair to her' – fact. This doesn't mean that you're accepting the logical implication of their emotion; for example, 'I deserve my child's anger', 'It's right to hit someone', 'It's okay for my child to lie to me', 'I have been unfair to her'. These interpretations are necessarily evaluative; they are judgements of our child or ourselves, (often extraordinarily understandable ones) based on the emotion our child is presenting, but they are not facts. Interpreting them in this way can result in defensive reactions, which can lead to disconnection. Therefore, if we truly accept emotions (our own and those of our children), and curiously wonder about them, we can often find out more than if we asked directly.

Most crucially, I am not asking you to abandon your judgements, but if you can suspend them it will help you to understand what is going on for your child, reconnect with them and stand a chance of working out a solution to the problem together.

Empathy

Hand in hand with acceptance comes empathy. Put simply, empathy is the ability and willingness to feel a little bit of what someone else is feeling. If we can accept a child's feelings, it is so much easier to feel empathic, and vice versa; if we can enter into a child's emotional world via empathy, we can often find it easier to accept their emotional states. Communication of our empathic understanding to our children enables them to integrate the idea that their inner world is understandable, that it can exist somewhere other than themselves and shame can begin to dissipate.

Get curious

Wrinkle your forehead, furrow your brow, and get comfortable with saying 'I wonder if/why/how...' This, in a nutshell, is how to do curiosity. When we use curiosity alongside acceptance and empathy, we can then hope our children will come up with some constructive things to say about what is going on for them. However, they may well not do that. They may reject our attempts to understand via dismissal, provocation or mockery. This doesn't mean we haven't been helpful or we're not on the right track. It most often means that the experience of someone entering our child's inner world is alien to them and they are suspicious of it. So, whilst we proceed respectfully and sensitively, we continue to try and share the burden of the trauma landscape they carry with them.

Sometimes being curious and empathic (via empathic commentary) is enough. We don't always need children to verbally engage in this exercise with us if they cannot; we simply continue to give them repeated experiences of being and feeling understood. This is a huge step and a momentous experience for children who have been isolated with their trauma, both externally by the people who surround them and internally by the pain of their own inner world.

Focus on emotion and connection

Successfully exploring 'why?' can also be helped by simply settling in and trying to connect with our children. This means dropping the focus on behaviour and instead focusing on feelings. Perhaps start by doing something you think might bring you closer together with your child regardless of whether it addresses the problem you and your child are currently confronted with. If you are connected and your child feels relaxed in your company, you are much more likely to be able to deal with the tricky issue together without upset and further fall-out. Your child is much more likely to be able to drop their shame and defences and thus their suspicions about your intentions and be more honest with you.

The inner negotiator

In therapeutic parenting we are trying to channel the inner negotiator rather than the police officer. We are collecting together all the elements listed above to approach our children, their experiences and their behaviours in a joining, collaborative way, one in which we can explore and understand our shared experiences and relationship.

✸ GRACIE AND JASON

Gracie is five. She has lived with her adoptive mum, Anne, and dad, Jason, since she was six months old. She is at home with her dad whilst her mum visits a poorly relative one Saturday. Gracie and her dad have eaten lunch together having had a busy morning of playing dressing up and doing some household jobs. They've had some fun but, as is reasonably common for Gracie at the moment, she seems hypersensitive to bumps and everything seems to be upsetting her.

Jason goes to empty the washing machine whilst Gracie continues to play. The next thing Jason hears is Gracie shouting and screaming something that he can't quite make sense of. He goes to Gracie and finds that she is sobbing, face down on the floor; her princess tiara is smashed next to her and there is black felt-tip scribbled all over her Elsa dress.

Reality: the exhausted Hare	Traditional: evaluation	Therapeutic: exploring 'why?'
✗	✗	✓
(Unpredictable)	(Not trauma-informed)	(Trauma-informed)

Comparison of approaches

Reality: the exhausted Hare
Approach

Before we start to think about what traditional and then therapeutic (EBM) approaches would encourage us to do in response to Gracie, let's explore what our instinctive, impulsive Hare system decision-making might lead us to do. Remember that this could be any one of us and is, in fact, all of us at one point or another.

In the moment, it is very likely that Jason would feel quite shocked but also weary with the demanding morning he's had. When he sees the broken and spoiled toys, he's likely to have an angry reaction. He might also see Gracie's upset and want to comfort her, but feel simultaneously frustrated with her. It feels to Jason like Gracie is too emotional and the 'overreactions' are irritating him.

On hearing Gracie, Jason sighs, puts the laundry down and walks through to the lounge where Gracie is. 'What's up now, Gracie?' he says, sounding exhausted. Gracie continues to sob and wail. She throws the shoe she has in her hand at the wall, and it knocks some more toys down onto the floor with a crash. 'For goodness sake, Gracie! What did you do that for! Look at the state of your dress! You love that dress!' He walks out of the room in frustration and gathers himself. The smashing and crashing resume. Jason goes back to Gracie and stands at the door again, 'HEY! STOP! What on earth is going on, Gracie? Why would you spoil your dressing up things?!' Gracie continues as she was. 'You were playing quite happily until I went out. Now you've started breaking everything! You just can't behave like this.' Gracie is unmoved and continues. 'Do you want a cuddle? Okay, well I'm fed up with this, I'll be in the kitchen when you've calmed down.'

Techniques

The 'techniques' (kind of) that Jason, our poor exhausted Hare, might use, could be something like the following:

- There is a pretty quick assumption about what has happened, that Gracie has 'lost it' and destroyed her toys in anger.

- Jason instinctively shows Gracie that he's fed up, with his grumpy, exhausted tone of voice; on some level he hopes this might make her behave 'better'.
- Jason shows he's angry and shocked, to let her know what she has done is out of order.
- There is an attempt by Jason to make sense of what has happened: 'Why did you do that?'
- Jason conveys to Gracie that what she has done is unacceptable to him.
- Jason communicates to Gracie that she is overreacting and needs to gather herself.
- There is an attempt to offer comfort.
- Jason puts in place a casual consequence: 'You can talk to me when you're calm.'

Traditional: evaluation (reward–punishment)
Approach
From this approach we view the priority as deterring Gracie from screaming and shouting and destroying her toys again. This textbook approach might discourage parents and carers from acting emotionally and apply the consequence that had been previously agreed on. This would necessarily involve evaluating Gracie's behaviour as unacceptable and acting to deter that behaviour.

Techniques

- We can try to investigate what caused the damage: was it an accident or was it deliberate?
- Having minimal interaction with Gracie so as not to reward 'negative behaviour', possibly involving leaving the room.
- Jason might move objects away to prevent Gracie from hurting herself.
- Jason would set a clear expectation: 'Come and talk to me when you're calm.'

- There would be clear consequences for breaking toys: 'No more dressing up today.'
- A reward chart could be put in place whereby Gracie would get a sticker for every day that goes by without a toy being broken.

Therapeutic: exploring 'why?' (EBM)
Approach

A therapeutic (EBM) approach to this situation would be to focus on understanding Gracie and the emotions that have got her to this place over evaluation of her and her behaviour. In order to do this, it is, as ever, crucial that we apply understanding and not evaluation to the *adults* too. So the first thing to remember about the EBM approach is that Jason will have to prioritize forgiving himself if (when!) he defaults to his Hare system reactions, which are not likely to be very understanding.

Techniques

- Jason is given full permission to feel irritated or whatever it is that he feels – overwhelmed, angry, tearful, exasperated, etc.
- Jason would be encouraged to regulate himself if he can, and to go to Gracie prepared to try and understand rather than evaluate her and her behaviour.
- Gracie would be approached with playfulness, acceptance, curiosity and empathy (PACE,[54, 55, 56] see above).
- Any objects that might be a safety hazard (if thrown, for example) would be cleared out of the way for Gracie and Jason's safety, and also to prevent Gracie from doing something that will be very likely to make Jason feel very angry, thus reducing the connection between them.
- We would think about physical proximity and non-verbal communication. Jason could express with his body that he is invested in taking the time to understand – sitting down on the floor beside Gracie and getting comfortable.

- Jason would show care and concern (also using empathy and acceptance): 'Oh, sweetheart! What on earth has made you feel like this?! It must be something really big to make you do that to your dress – you love that dress!'

- We could invite (but not expect) a two-way conversation: 'I wonder what's going on...maybe you're missing Mum...or you feel like you wanted me to carry on playing when I went to sort the washing... I'm not sure what it is, but I do know something's going on for you.'

- We can offer a way out with no shame:
  - Playfulness can often help with this to change the mood in the room: 'Oh no! You've made a great big snot puddle on the floor! Watch out! Don't slip on it! Oh no! Aargh! I might slip – aargh!'
  - Once Gracie is a little calmer, Jason could suggest some alternative activity for them: 'Want to help me fold the washing?' or 'I think we're getting all stressed, so let's have a sit down and a snack.'

- Concentrating on exploring 'why?' doesn't mean that there is never a need for evaluation or consequences, but it is the gateway to reconnection and holds the potential for cooperation on solving problems or trying to prevent them.

Let's get practical
Self-regulation

The first step in enabling yourself to explore 'why?' and not evaluate is self-regulation. If you act based on your frustration, irritation, worry, etc. you are, of necessity, going to be acting in an emotionally unregulated way. In times of trouble, a developmentally traumatized child will struggle more than anyone with their ability to regulate their feelings, and needs you to be their external hard drive, someone they can use to regulate themselves. This means they need you to be as regulated as you can be.

There's a meme doing the rounds on social media that goes something like 'When children are overwhelmed by big feelings, it's our job to share our calm, not join in their chaos'. It's a great message.

However, what it misses is an understanding of how difficult that can be, especially when our buttons are pressed by children expressing their trauma.

Being okay with getting it wrong

So how can we regulate our emotions to help our children regulate theirs? Well, first of all, we won't be able to all the time, and we have to get comfortable with that. Trying hard will help but it won't mean that you'll succeed every single time in staying calm and regulated. So, get used to forgiving yourself and working out how to repair your relationship with your child. In an ideal world, start the repair by labelling (in a contained way) how you struggled in that moment and apologize, if you can, for not being able to help them right there and then. For example, 'Oh, sweetheart, we got ourselves into a huge mess then, didn't we? You needed me to understand and help you with your feelings and I got angry and shouted instead! I think my feelings got big too. I'm so sorry. Can I try and help now?'

Ways of regulating

Sometimes simply understanding how we can be useful by regulating our children can snap us into the right frame of mind, but not always...

Grounding

Sometimes a sensory experience can take us away from tricky feelings and help us to come back to the rational bits of our brain and our Tortoise decision-making system. There is a comprehensive discussion of grounding with lots of examples and guidance in Superpower #1: Parental Self-Acceptance.

Mindfulness

What is mindfulness? Mindfulness is the practice of accepting but simultaneously letting go of negative thoughts and emotions.

An analogy that many parents and carers have found useful has been to imagine their thoughts and feelings as a loud radio, whose broadcast is invasive and preoccupying. Much of the time, people deal with these thoughts and feelings by trying to control them – we turn the radio off to silence the preoccupying thoughts and feelings. The problem with this approach is that it becomes preoccupying in itself. This kind of judgemental attitude towards our inner worlds leads to preoccupying *worry about worry* or *sadness about sadness*. We end up being constantly vigilant for thoughts or feelings we don't want – it's the classic 'don't think about a pink elephant' thought experiment. (If you haven't heard about this, give it a try. Close your eyes and take two minutes. You must definitely NOT think of a pink elephant.) Put simply, it's pretty impossible not to focus on things that are looming large for us, no matter how hard we try.

The objective in mindfulness is to be 'mindful' of your inner world, to observe it, describe it and accept it. In achieving this we turn the volume of our metaphorical radios down. We accept the presence of the radio, but we can choose whether or not we attend to it, and perhaps even which station we'd like to listen to. Alternatively, you may get to a stage where you can *lean into* your feelings. Perhaps when you observe your anger for your child, you can look at it as a vulnerable, innocent part of yourself that needs nurturing.

Mindfulness is not something we can dive into and be good at straightaway. It takes practice, and so I recommend taking at least five minutes a day to hone and sustain your mindfulness muscles.

Why is mindfulness particularly helpful for foster carers and adopters (and other professionals working with relationship trauma)?

Parenting children whose characters have been formed in environments of neglect and/or abuse exposes foster carers and adopters to some of the most intense and traumatizing thoughts and feelings there are. Therefore, a strategy for dealing with them is not only essential for the adults but also to help prevent those difficult thoughts and feelings spilling back into their relationship with their child.

Another very important reason why mindfulness can be helpful for foster carers and adopters is that it promotes self-acceptance and a non-judgemental attitude towards our inner worlds. Getting into this mindset for ourselves is the first step towards being able to do the same for the very difficult thoughts, feelings and behaviours of traumatized children.

Anyone exposed to the relational dynamics inherent in traumatizing abuse and/or neglect can benefit from the self-acceptance and self-awareness that mindfulness practice can bring. So, social workers, teachers and therapists might just like to indulge themselves in the world of mindfulness too.

An example of mindfulness practice

You might like to record yourself talking through the mindfulness session so you can play it back to yourself rather than worrying about remembering what to do. Alternatively, just read this section through several times and remember the main themes of the practice session.

Set yourself a time when you can be quiet and undistracted. Get yourself comfy in a relaxed but alert position. Sitting in a comfortable chair is ideal.

1. Begin by drawing your attention to what you are experiencing right now. What thoughts are around? What feelings are around? What can you feel in your body? Notice all of these internal experiences. Don't judge them; don't fight them. Try describing them to yourself and then watch them float away. Notice as other thoughts, feelings and sensations come, and watch them float away again. Do this for around 90 seconds. (If you're recording this to play back to yourself, repeat these instructions for the 90 seconds.)

2. Now take your focus to the sensation of your breath in your belly. Concentrate on how your belly feels as you take a slow, deep breath in, and again, as you breathe out. If thoughts or feelings come along, observe them and focus back on the feelings of your breath. As you breathe out, let all of the thoughts and feelings go. Try saying to yourself, 'It's okay, let go', as you breathe out. Spend around 90 seconds doing this.

3. Now broaden your focus to the experience of your breath in your whole body. Notice each area of your body and how it feels as you breathe in and then out, deeply and slowly. If there are any strong feelings, thoughts or sensations around,

don't judge yourself for them. Try saying to yourself, 'That's okay, just let me feel it', and then focus back on the sensations of your breath in your body. Do this for around 90 seconds.

As you practice this more and more, you may like to extend the amount of time you spend on each of the three sections of this practice.

Reading between the lines (reading the emotion)

Often, when we're trying to understand rather than evaluate, we need to be able to close our ears to the minutiae of what is being said. This doesn't mean we ignore what our children are telling us, but that we need to listen to the verbal *and* the non-verbal communication. You will have had countless experiences of seeing a child distressed or angry, and when you ask them what is wrong, they may deny their upset or put it down to some small incongruent event that just doesn't match the enormity of the response. This can mean that your child has had a bigger issue triggered by, for example, not having a chocolate biscuit before dinner. It could also mean that they are using a 'post-hoc rationalization' (see Superpower #1: Parental Self-Acceptance), that is, 'gut reaction first, work out the reasons later', that they just have the feeling and don't know why, so they set about trying to justify their reaction in a way that might make sense to you and to themselves.

At these times, when there is little apparent sense to our children's emotions, our job is to accept that we need to help them by making sense, honestly and authentically, of what they might be feeling. This means looking at the bigger picture. If a child reacts to the frustration of not being able to find their shoe by having a complete meltdown and throwing things and blaming you, this is about more than a missing shoe. Reading between the emotional lines, it could be about a struggle to regulate feelings or the feelings that loss brings about or the feelings brought about by the chaos of not finding their things and/or a sensory memory of past consequences for losing something, etc. A good way to verbalize this in the moment would be something like 'Losing your shoe feels like a really big deal!' Later on, you might be able to make a bigger link: 'You got so upset and angry when you lost your shoe. It felt like such a big deal to you! I was just trying to get my head around why it felt so important. Perhaps because you were really beating yourself up about it and you're used to grown-ups getting really angry about stuff like that.'

Empathic commentary

When you're trying to understand and not evaluate your child and their behaviour, empathic commentary can be a really useful technique. I give the golden rules for empathic commentary in *Why Can't My Child Behave?*, but if you read the examples in this book, you'll get the idea. Remember these statements might not lead into a two-way conversation, and that's okay. You are helping to give shape and organization to a chaotic inner world, just by noticing and making good guesses about what's going on. Once you've got the hang of it, you can adapt these to make them sound more like you and not me. Here are some examples to give you some ideas:

- 'Oh goodness, something is going on for you! Can we try and work it out together?'
- 'I wonder how trying to hit me then made sense to you. I know that you know what a bad idea hitting is. Let's work it out.'
- 'It feels really bad to you when I talk to someone else on the phone. I wonder what that makes you feel. Perhaps it makes you feel left out or lonely.'
- 'Me asking you to make your bed makes you really angry. Hmmm, I wonder why that is... Maybe it's the idea that an adult is trying to force you to do something.'

Story-telling tone

The way in which you explore and try to understand is very important. It can be enormously powerful to feed back small chunks of understanding of your child's inner world. Your tone of voice can be very powerful in doing this. I've taken this concept from Dan Hughes' work on Dyadic Developmental Psychotherapy (DDP).[57]

A story-telling tone is a light, rhythmical, almost melodic, way of using your voice. It can also be a very animated way of speaking, just like the tone you'd use when reading a storybook out loud.

Examples of using a story-telling tone include:

- 'Oh! So, you were talking to Dad and you got this big ball of angry in your tummy and it burst out in a smashy, crashy way!'
- 'So, you were talking to Joe and he said something about his family and you suddenly felt really lonely and lost and then you haven't wanted to talk to anyone.'
- 'Right, so you were just minding your own business, trying to stay out of trouble, but you knew you were feeling fragile and then, boom! Everyone rushed down the corridor and you got completely overwhelmed! It's no wonder you started pushing and shoving your way out of there!'

The focus on understanding over evaluation is inextricably linked with the debate about the relative importance of emotional acceptance and behavioural change, which will be the subject of our next chapter.

BEHAVIOURAL CHANGE VS. EMOTIONAL ACCEPTANCE

Introduction

In this chapter we will explore emotional acceptance as a therapeutic alternative to the traditional focus on behaviour change.

Generally, parenting advice focuses adults on what they should do to change and shape the behaviour of their children. At times, however, there is a merit and, indeed, an emotional and pragmatic need, to stop overtly trying to change it and start trying to work through acceptance.

Acceptance in this context means prioritizing understanding our children's motivations and validating their inner world just as it is. This allows us to reduce shame and build connection, thus reducing the need for trauma-driven behavioural challenges.

There are a few parts to this idea, but the first thing to say is that it is not simply a matter of 'giving up' or letting children 'get away with' behaviour that hurts, upsets or offends our sense of what is right and good behaviour. Parenting empathically does not mean parenting permissively.

An alternative way of thinking about this chapter might be to compare the reward–punishment message of 'nip it in the bud' with an acceptance-based approach of 'don't sweat the small stuff'. The 'nip it in the bud' mentality carries connotations that nothing should be missed, that all problematic behaviour must be swiftly and decisively acted on so that it doesn't grow into something huge and unmanageable. Alternatively, taking a 'don't sweat the small stuff' approach focuses us on regulating our reactions first, and working out whether anything needs to change, or perhaps, more realistically, whether it can be changed. It buys us time and space and helps us to focus on a calm, regulated approach so we can impart this to our children. It also means that we don't exhaust ourselves over things that aren't crucial or those things that we stand little chance of changing.

Behavioural change in reward–punishment thinking
What if we are trying to change a behaviour that helps our child?

Many of the things that we struggle with in our children's behaviour are there for good reason. They may well have been survival strategies that worked well for them but now cause them troubles. For example, a child who moves quickly to rage may have bought himself crucial moments in an environment of physical violence, but he is chastised or punished in his new home. Or a young person who is avoidant of demands placed on them may save themselves from the emotional overwhelm of a needy parent but find themselves critiqued by their new emotionally available parents who expect more from them.

When we encounter a behaviour in our children that we find challenging or problematic, it's easy to default to the assumption that changing the behaviour is a simple matter of the child (and/or parent) being more disciplined. This leads parents to seeing their role as teaching children to work hard and ignore what their survival instinct tells them, to help children to overcome their 'incorrect' defaults and be different. Sometimes, rather than changing the survival instinct it is more effective and certainly more connecting to adjust our behaviour and accept why that behaviour needs to be there.

Examples of trauma behaviour that 'helps'

Behaviour that 'helps'	How it may have helped in the past (this list is not exhaustive – there may be many other explanations)
Explosive anger	Buying crucial minutes to get away from a physical attack
Poor hygiene	Deterring a sexual abuser
Frequent masturbation	Soothing unmanageable feelings or stimulation at a time of mental shut-down
Sending sexual images	Creating a desperately longed-for connection
Stealing	Undermining a relationship that may be assumed (based on past experience) to be intrusive or coercive
Lying	Disrupting an emerging trust in a relationship (when trust has made a child vulnerable in the past)
Aloofness	Keeping distance from an adult who may overwhelm the child with excessive need
Helping 'too much'	Ensuring that a child is not forgotten

The emotional acceptance mindset gears us up to accept that many default, instinctive behaviours have become programmed because they saved our child's life, time and time again. Or they gave them desperately longed-for comfort at a time of crippling loneliness. Alternatively, they are impulses that convulse through our child's body before they even knew what was happening.

If that is the case and we focus solely on changing behaviour, what happens? How would it feel to be on the receiving end of rewards and consequences from the most significant person in our lives to change a behaviour that has such huge significance to us? Huge significance because it helps us feel less lonely or more confident and connected. I can only imagine it would have huge ramifications for what I thought about myself, the adult involved and the world at large. It would also be likely to trigger a defensive bounce-back from those unmanageable thoughts.

I might think about myself:

- 'What's wrong with me for wanting to do that so badly?'

- 'Am I weird because the thing I need to do most is so awful to my mum?'

It might make me think about my most important grown-up:

- 'How could they try and stop me doing something so important?'
- 'Why do they want me to stop the only thing that helps me when I'm terrified/lonely/angry?!'

And I might think about how the rest of the world sees me:

- 'I don't fit in.'
- 'They think I'm a freak.'
- 'They think I'm disgusting.'
- 'They look at me like I'm nasty.'
- 'No one else feels like I do.'
- 'How horrible must people think I am if everyone is so desperate for me to change?'

It's really no wonder that we meet resistance from children when we try to change their trauma-based behaviours. The reaction is the same as we would expect if we were telling, reprimanding or cajoling and manipulating our children to stay put when faced with a raging fire that they *know* in their core they must escape.

If you can, take a moment to think about something you might do to survive or make a truly (psychologically or physically) dangerous situation survivable. For example, to overcome loneliness or fear, you might keep the TV or radio on when you're alone in the house. Or to avoid feeling vulnerable or frightened walking home from work at night, you might carry a personal alarm or talk to someone on the phone. Imagine, then, that someone more powerful than you insists that you stop doing that thing, and uses their power to force you to sit at home with your fear in silence or takes away your personal alarm.

We also need to consider the implications of success. If we do manage to change a child's behaviour, without understanding its underlying causes, what do we leave behind? What sense could any of us make of the chaotic psychological jumble we are left with when we are forced to override, through discipline, our drives to survive? Using the examples above, if we must give up the comfort of the TV, we are left feeling frightened and alone. If we are stopped from calling someone on our walk home, we are left with panic and vulnerability.

A more sensitive approach to tackling these survival strategies when they cause our children (and/or us) damage in some way will come somewhat more naturally when we understand ways in which they 'help'. For example, when we look at compulsive masturbation as just a 'problem behaviour', we simply use rewards and punishments to make it stop. However, the need that caused it, for example, for emotional regulation, will then require a different solution, perhaps self-harm or alcohol use. However, when we view that same issue with a full understanding of how it 'helps', we provide a solution for the emotional regulation, such as diverting our child to positive regulation, talking to us when they can or a sensory activity such as playing with Play-Doh® or jumping on a trampoline.

Throughout this book I talk about therapeutic parenting and EBM as a way to respond to 'trauma-based' behaviours. However, by engaging emotionally, sensitively and with an awareness of a child's internal world, we are optimizing the ability to connect and supporting the mental health of all children, regardless of what 'behaviours' or parts of themselves they are showing us. We don't, therefore, need to pick apart what is 'trauma-based' behaviour and what isn't; if we are engaged, empathic and trying to understand, we cannot do any harm.

How reward–punishment thinking can discourage children's real insight into 'why?'

One of the greatest dangers, when we focus on behavioural change, is that we actively train children not to develop an understanding of why they behave the way they do. People who have experienced developmental trauma typically struggle more with reflecting on their inner worlds than others (although this is not, of course, exclusive to those of us who have experienced trauma). Continuing to focus on behaviour rather than children's inner worlds only serves to make this worse. One of the factors that is known to protect children from later complex mental health issues is good reflective functioning (for example, being able to think about one's own behaviour either in the moment or later on without defensiveness).[58] It is crucial, therefore, in our parenting of developmentally traumatized children, that we prioritize authentic insights (that is, realistic, empathic ideas about why they may do something rather than defaulting to easy but insubstantial ideas about naughtiness, such as 'My child is feeling the need to be in control right now' or 'My child is feeling angry right now, even though that anger doesn't seem justified to me') into the 'whys' of their behaviour rather than just enabling them to be 'good' children.

If we focus only, or primarily, on changing behaviour, we may not be helping them to stop a 'problem behaviour' but rather 'training' them to tell us they've stopped when they really can't. We may therefore be teaching our children to lie to us. We also, inadvertently, encourage the 'gut reaction first, think up the reasons later' (post-hoc rationalizations, discussed in Superpower #1: Parental Self-Acceptance). This can encourage children to create false narratives that are at best frustrating and at worst infuriating for us. For children, this can expand and crystalize a sense of not being connected with their inner worlds. Conversely, if we strive to understand our children's inner worlds and enable them to do the same, we discourage shame and the consequent need to lie about their shame-inducing behaviour.

Our children are already programmed by experience of abuse and/or neglect to deny their inner worlds (see the section on 'Shame' in the book's Introduction). However, if we can retrain ourselves, and ultimately them, to accept and understand the drives from their inner world, we can jointly invest in understanding the problem and then the solution.

Being seen to do the 'right' thing

The pressures of expectation often drive us as parents and carers to do what we feel others think we should do rather than what we want to do. Many parents feel that they need to address behaviours that may not bother them too much, but about which they feel judged by grandparents, friends, other parents at the school gates, etc. In the case of foster carers there is the massive additional pressure from other professionals who may not be up to speed with therapeutic approaches to parenting.

The pressure of this shouldn't be under-estimated; it's huge! It can often happen without parents realizing, too. When so much planning has gone into being a parent, as it so often has for foster carers and adopters, being seen to be 'good' at it takes on a whole new level of importance.

What do we mean by emotional acceptance?
Adults first
One of the key elements that is so, so hard to remember when parents and carers are in the thick of it, is that we must apply the principle of emotional acceptance to ourselves first. Doing so enables us to override our Hare system, to slowly and deliberately take back control of ourselves and engage a deliberate strategy in reaction to our own wellbeing and our therapeutic parenting.

If we don't try to accept ourselves, we are far more vulnerable to acting on impulse, reacting defensively, repeating trauma patterns that children bring with them and/or creating a narrative that explains how we behave but doesn't deepen understanding ('gut reaction first, think up the reasons later'). Take a look back at Superpower #1: Parental Self-Acceptance for a full exploration of the need for parental self-acceptance and our unhelpful tendency to rely on fragile self-discipline.

If we plan and practice and persevere with acceptance of ourselves, we then set the scene for acceptance, and prime ourselves to accept the emotional state of our children when we need to.

Acceptance as self-preservation
So much of my face-to-face work with parents and children, when their families are in crisis, comes down to a question of self-preservation. When relationships, even family stability, are at

breaking point, the mental health of all people concerned has severely deteriorated and no one can see any good enough way out – at points such as these, when all attempts to change behaviour quickly, using whatever means available, have failed, the biggest question in the room is 'Can you find a way to accept yourself and your child just the way you are?' It is the very toughest of questions, but it tends to be one that begins to crack through to a different mindset, facilitating a complete paradigm shift. If this way of thinking is possible, we can often start to move from exhausting, and usually fruitless, efforts to change our own and our children's behaviour towards a state of being in which we can achieve some stillness to reflect and join with our child. In dropping the star charts, grounding and incessant invitations to conflict, we can sometimes break through to defeat the common enemy of disconnection and adversarial isolation.

Acceptance as an indirect route to behaviour change

Opening the doors to acceptance and abandoning direct attempts to change behaviour doesn't necessarily mean that change will not come, but it does mean accepting that it is a longer process. We can change habits with star charts, but to change minds we need empathy, and that takes time.

Once we have changed the focus from behaviour change to emotional acceptance, we are better able to relax and accept the status quo. The conflict between us as parents and carers and our behaviourally challenging children can then be turned to curiosity and an atmosphere in which our children are more likely to unite with us to battle the impacts of their trauma on themselves and us.

Many of our own behaviours would benefit from acceptance. These are the things that we don't want to do but do compulsively, experiencing very little sense of choice about them, such as smoking, eating too much or shouting at our children. They are also things that we are shamed and condemned by others and ourselves for which. This shame is likely to trigger defensive and dissociative reactions (when we psychologically and unconsciously distance ourselves from what we've done because it feels too awful), which diminishes our ability to take responsibility for solving the problem.

The link between 'happiness' and 'goodness'

'Be a good girl.' 'Make sure you're good for your Nan.' 'Well done! You were such a good boy at the shops.' We still hear people ask new parents, 'Is he a good baby, does he sleep through the night?' When we pick it apart, 'goodness' is really quite a strange concept to apply to children. It implies that all of the behaviour of children and babies is a choice and is entirely within their control. This may be true of some behaviour, that we may use our slow, deliberate Tortoise system to 'choose' a way of being. However, this fails to take into account that most of our decisions are made using our impulsive Hare system and the emotional rivers that might push and pull us to behave in certain ways in reaction to any given situation. It certainly massively underestimates the impact on mental state and behaviour that past trauma, particularly trauma that has relationships as its very fabric, has on a person's ability to be 'good'.

Let's phrase it slightly differently. When you are grumpy, sad, depressed, irritated or downright furious, how cooperative are you with the people you love? Is it fair that you are disciplined and criticized for your reactions? Maybe some will say it is. But the crucial question is, does that discipline and criticism make you feel or behave differently? Does the discipline and criticism make you less grumpy, sad, depressed, irritated or downright furious? Chances are it will actually make those things worse. If you struggle to regulate those uncomfortable emotions, it's also likely to make you less cooperative and kind to your loved ones.

It comes down to this – on the link between happiness and goodness, happier, more connected children (and adults) are likely to be more invested in doing things that make other people happier, contributing to cooperative family life.

We want our children to be happy, so seeing them unhappy is very tough to handle. We can fall into the trap of disciplining bad behaviours (which may be indicative of unhappiness) because we want to escape from the idea of our children as unhappy. Clearly, however, addressing behaviour in this way may make children behave 'better', but it is very unlikely to really make them happier.

Conversely, if we abandon our focus on the 'goodness' of behaviour and redirect ourselves to connection and emotional acceptance, we are more likely (but not guaranteed) to see the seeds of happiness and therefore positive participation in relationships.

Focus on connection

Connecting emotionally and meaningfully with our traumatized children is such a helpful strategy to move us towards emotional acceptance. Asking yourself, after a tricky behaviour, how you could have got to that place and what your child must have *felt* for that way of doing things to have made sense can be a powerful tool in connecting to your child and thus accepting the emotional predicament they have found themselves in.

The difference between emotional acceptance and behavioural acceptance

Once we are attuned and can accurately pick apart emotions from their consequent behaviours, we can see that there is a clear line between the two, and that one can be accepted independently of the other. It is possible to observe and accept an emotional state of distress or anger (in yourself or in your child), but to think and feel that hitting someone is not okay. It is, in fact, very important that we work hard to acknowledge, and aim to stop, any behaviour that hurts anyone, emotionally or physically.

✳ OLI, RICHARD AND TIM

Oli is 17 and lives with his adoptive dads, Richard and Tim. Oli had an early history of extreme neglect whereby he was left entirely by himself for long stretches of time. When adults were around, they did not attend to him, either physically or emotionally. Oli has a part-time job in a supermarket, but he only gets a few shifts here and there. He hasn't had any shifts for three weeks. Oli has recently split up with his girlfriend. He's generally coping pretty well but has had periods of depression. He has a history of becoming rageful with his dads when he gets overwhelmed, but it hasn't happened that often, until recently.

During these rages Oli will shout aggressively and has thrown things and smashed crockery in the past. Oli smokes cigarettes and struggles to manage his mood and rages when he doesn't have them. Due to his current lack of funds, he constantly asks Richard and Tim for money to buy cigarettes. They don't like Oli smoking, primarily because of the damage it does his health, but also, they simply don't like the smell on Oli and in the house.

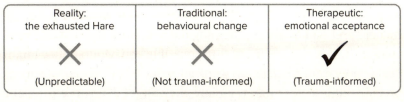

Comparison of approaches

Reality: the exhausted Hare
Approach
Before we start to think about what traditional and then EBM approaches would encourage us to do in response to Oli, let's explore what our instinctive, impulsive Hare system decision-making might lead us to do. Remember that this characterization represents any one of us and at one point or another, probably covers *all* of us.

Techniques
The things that Richard and Tim, our poor exhausted Hares, might use could be something like the following:

- Trying to exert discipline, control and protection: 'No, Oli, you're not having any money! You're going to spend it on cigarettes. You know I hate you smoking! Besides that, I'm not going to give you money after you've been shouting at us and pushing me around for the last hour! How dare you even ask!'
- Placating Oli, to try and keep the peace whilst simultaneously dealing with their sense that they are doing the wrong thing: 'Oh for God's sake just have it. I don't care anymore, just do what you like and leave us alone!'

- Avoiding conflict: going out of the house or keeping their distance from Oli.

Traditional: behavioural change (reward–punishment)

Approach

A traditional, reward–punishment approach would encourage Richard and Tim to start by defining the behaviour they would like to change. In this case there are three possible behaviours. They might decide they want to deter Oli from smoking. They may equally focus on Oli's requests for money. Finally, they might define the 'problem' as the angry outbursts that happen when they decide not to give Oli money.

Techniques

Oli's requests for money might be treated with:

- Consistent, calm, simple messages to decline his requests.
- No further elaboration on the matter with which they disagree – not entering into lengthy discussion and debate (which might lead to conflict).

Oli's consequent rage could be met with:

- No debate and discussion with Oli about how fair it is or whether they should change their minds.
- Consequences being laid down in response to Oli's apparent attempts to intimidate his parents.

Oli's positive attempts to deal with the problematic issues, such as not asking for money, talking calmly about alternative solutions, would be met with:

- Praise.
- Support.
- Other tangible rewards.

Therapeutic: emotional acceptance (EBM)

Approach

This is a prime example of when acceptance needs to start with the adults. Richard and Tim are feeling ashamed of themselves for letting their vulnerable child have something that harms him. They are also feeling ineffectual as parents because they are setting a boundary and then 'giving in'. In addition to all that, they are all more disconnected from one another than ever. They are also feeling frightened and out of control with regard to Oli's rages. Emotional acceptance, for these parents, means taking a step back and accepting that they are simply doing the best they can in the situation they are faced with. Wouldn't we all struggle with this particular set of circumstances?!

Once Tim and Richard have regulated themselves and accepted their own reaction to all of this, they might be able to explore the possibility of accepting Oli's emotions at these times.

Oli is clearly becoming disproportionately (to our eyes) upset and aggressive to his parents at these times. This could be due to a physiological addiction to nicotine, but there are also likely to be psychological and emotional factors at play that explain the extremity of his reaction. How does being dependent on his parents, when faced with a physiological need, feel for Oli? We can only imagine the lengths Oli will have been to in order to get his needs met as a baby and young child in an environment when no adult was available to him. It's tough to contemplate the hours he will have cried and screamed for help, the rage and despair he will have faced time and time again. Now, aged 17, and dependent on people for something that his body is crying out for, that they refuse to allow him to have, he will be transported back to those feelings he lived with for so long in his early years. He will unconsciously default to the same extreme strategies that he needed to get him through his early years: 'I must get my needs met by any means necessary.'

Ultimately, as with many trauma behaviours, there is no clear, easy solution for Richard and Tim. They are faced with the need to simultaneously accept the tremendous pain that Oli is thrown back into by this situation and their need to protect his physical health.

Techniques

For the parents:

- First and foremost, no matter what approach you're using, safety must come first. So if there was a risk that Oli might hurt himself, his parents or anyone else, then that risk needs to be managed first. This might possibly mean one of his parents leaving the house, calling the police or taking Oli to A&E.
- Richard and Tim could, in this situation, imagine how they would talk to a friend in a similar situation. Would they judge their friend as harshly as they are judging themselves?
- They could talk to other adopters who may be able to empathize and not judge.
- They may also want to try mindfulness (see Superpower #6: Exploring 'Why?').
- It may be that grounding techniques would help (see Superpower #1: Parental Self-Acceptance).
- They could try to establish clarity for themselves about the no-win situation. There is no one, consistent rule that will work in this situation, and they will need to reconcile themselves to that.
- It would be helpful for Richard and Tim to establish clarity about their multiple roles in this situation and be clear about the number of things they are trying to safeguard:
  - Oli's physical health.
  - Compassion for Oli's early trauma and the enormous dysregulation it can cause in the present.
  - Understanding the impact of Oli feeling dependent on his parents to meet these physical and emotional needs.
  - Protection of their relationship with Oli. This means taking their own feelings and needs in the parent–child relationship seriously as well as Oli's.

For Oli:

- Oli will need the family to have a clear conversation at a time of calm, following some time to connect. The conversation should cover the trickiness of the dilemma facing them all;

for example, 'We're so worried about you smoking because it harms your body, we care about you and we want to protect you. We see how stressed not having cigarettes makes you feel and how awful it is for you to have to depend on us. Us saying "no" to you makes you feel so desperate! Our job is to try and look after your body, your feelings *and* your relationship with us.'

- Richard and Tim will spend time with Oli wondering about what it feels like to him that they want to deny him the cigarettes: 'It makes you so angry with us when we say we're not going to help you get the cigarettes. I'm guessing you really hate us when we do that.'

- A judgement will need to be made by the parents on each occasion, about which is the element of protection that needs to be prioritized at that time. This will need calm negotiation with Oli. To help them make the right decision each time the issue arises, they could ask themselves the following questions:

  - Can Oli tolerate not having cigarettes for another day? In which case, they do not give him the money. They might try to distract him and nurture him with fun, relationally based activities together (that is, things they can do together, such as go to the cinema, play football in the garden, play computer games).

  - Do Oli's feelings of terror, telling him that his bodily needs will not be met, need to be nurtured on this occasion? Should understanding his rage about being dependent on adults when he unconsciously expects them to abuse and ignore him be prioritized? If so, the parents could talk gently and with acceptance about this, and see if they can find a way to nurture Oli and ground him in the safety of his present relationships. They could cook together, go to the shops together, watch a funny TV programme together, play football in the garden. They may or may not decide that giving him the money today is what Oli needs most. If Oli's parents decide that giving him money is the best solution today, then it is best done when everyone is feeling understood and well regulated.

- Does the relationship between Oli and his parents need to come first today? If so, they may give him money, calmly and without feeling defeated, knowing they will all get on so much better and maybe be able to plan for protecting his physical health on another occasion.

- Richard and Tim can then plan for the future with Oli. They will talk to Oli clearly about how their part of the interaction is likely to look: 'Every single time you ask for money, we're going to have to try and weigh up whether it's your body, your mind or our relationship that needs to be looked after most, and we'll work out the answers together each and every time.'

Let's get practical
Self-acceptance

It has hopefully become clear that acceptance is not just something to be given out to others; it is something to absorb and offer yourself. The ability to uncritically observe and accept one's own experiences, thoughts and feelings is as liberating as it is essential when parenting traumatized children.

It is certainly a different mindset than most of us are used to. The best, most practical way to get to a point of self-acceptance is to practise. Notice whenever you tell yourself off, criticize yourself or judge yourself harshly for something you've done. Practising mindfulness can be really helpful. This may sound very alien and heavy to some, but the practicalities of mindfulness are simply to sit in a room by yourself in peace and quiet for three to five minutes at a time. You can use apps to help you. Headspace[59] and Calm[60] are a couple of good ones. Also take a look at Superpower #1: Parental Self-Acceptance for a greater exploration of self-acceptance.

Behavioural containment

Managing the behaviour of our children therapeutically means focusing on the emotions that drive behaviour, more than the behaviours themselves. This doesn't mean that we ignore the behaviour. Ignoring behaviour that communicates something about our children's inner world is daft. We can use that behaviour to help us understand what is going on for our children. Some behaviours can be talked about slowly and in a considered way. Others, however, demand immediate action to stop them. This is not the same as punishing for 'bad' behaviour, if necessary. Behavioural containment means communicating with words and actions that the behaviour cannot continue. However, we don't do it in order to train or teach our child not to do it in the future. It is a here-and-now imperative rather than a teaching and learning exercise.

Behavioural containment means doing anything possible and necessary to stop a behaviour that is immediately harmful. For example, when your child is habitually kicking you under the table and asking them to stop hasn't worked, it may be necessary to take hold of their foot to prevent the next kick or to move out of the way. Whilst doing so, it is helpful to say something like 'I can't allow you to kick me again so I'll move your foot' or 'I'll move away from you so it can't happen again'. Ideally this can be done without anger. For a teenager who is leaving the house late at night and you believe they won't be safe, behavioural containment might be 'I can't allow you to go off on your own and make yourself unsafe so I will have to follow you/call your friends to find out where you are and bring you home' (called 'tailing' in Non-Violent Resistance Therapy, NVR, a form of systemic family therapy, which has been developed for aggressive, violent, controlling and self-destructive behaviour in young people[61]). For a child who is at risk due to posting naked pictures of themselves and sending them to others, you may need to contain that behaviour and say something like 'I can't allow you to be at risk in that way so I am going to have to take your phone away'.

Out of context these strategies can look very much like punishment; however, the motivation is to prevent the problem in the here and now, to increase parental presence and strengthen the relationship, *not* to teach a lesson. The delivery is also different. We maintain our gentle, calm, assertive empathy as we ensure safety for our children. There is a very big difference between 'Right, that's it, you need to stop sending pictures of yourself. You can't have your phone for a week!' and 'I'm sorry but I'm so worried about you. I can't allow you to send naked pictures of yourself so I'm going to have to take your phone away until we can make sure you are safe with a phone.'

Talking about behaviour: naming without blaming or shaming

Emotional acceptance involves accepting a whole person. This means acknowledging what is wonderful, and finding empathic understanding of challenging issues but *not* ignoring any ugly truths about difficult behaviour. We must not ignore challenging behaviour as doing so risks presenting a vision of the world for our child in which their trauma-based behaviour cannot even be named or acknowledged. We do not help our children by ignoring any aspect of their being, particularly those strong, often unconscious, communications about their inner worlds that we might find challenging to live with. However, we can acknowledge these behaviours without blaming our children for them or shaming children for what their trauma has landed them with.

Focusing on behavioural change rather than emotional acceptance typically leads us to talk about behaviour in a shaming way in line with thinking that reprimand and consequence will help children to stop behaving in ways we don't like.

There can also be some issues with the opposite approach. Adults who try dedicatedly to use empathic, therapeutic parenting can often fall into the kindly trap of focusing only on the lovely, likeable and endearing qualities of their children. This should most certainly come first, and builds trust and connection. However, it can serve to communicate to children that there are parts of them that are intolerable to us; that the only parts of them that are acceptable are their 'nicest' parts, and those bits of them that originate from and/ or communicate their trauma are unacceptable and unknowable. Emotional acceptance means knowing, understanding and even loving the toughest or simply the tooth-grindingly irritating parts too.

For example, let's take a child who bounces a balloon on your head as hard as they can whilst you're trying to talk to them about something serious. A super-tolerant person trying to parent empathically might make the mistake of ignoring the impact on them and talking about something else. To name without shame you might try: 'You're hitting me with that balloon. I wonder if you're trying to distract me from talking to you/really trying to make me cross with you.' Or you may need to intervene with behavioural containment before the relationship is jolted by a loss of temper. For example: 'Sweetheart, I don't like you hitting me with the balloon while I'm trying to talk. If you don't stop, I will have to take it away.'

With a young person who swears at you when you ask them to do the washing-up, you might try: 'You are shouting and swearing at me, and I feel pretty sure I haven't done anything do deserve it. I wonder what's going on for you to make that make sense.'

This also links with the importance of you as the responsible parent keeping your presence at home high and staying 'in charge' but discussing the impact on you of what your child does. This, of course, needs to be done in a very emotionally contained way in front of your child, and with empathy for why they might be doing it – something like 'I'm guessing there's a reason you're shouting at me, but it does really upset me'. The need to prioritize and protect the relationship between yourself and your child can also mean you may need to name without shame: 'I'm finding the way we're interacting today really hard; the fact that you're shouting at me and that I'm snapping back at you. I'm going to take half an hour out for me, so we don't fall out today. That's going to be better for both of us. I love you.'

How to protect your relationship

It can be helpful, when grappling with tough questions around challenging behaviour, to change focus from the need to be a disciplinarian to the need to protect the relationship between you and your child (and, in fact, your child's relationships with others).

So, when faced with very tangible questions about what approach you should take in relation to a particular problem, such as 'Should I distance myself or try to comfort my child when she is screaming in my face and it makes me angry?', the crucial question to ask, with as much acceptance and tolerance of both yourself and your child as you can muster, is 'Which of the two potential courses of action (staying to comfort her but getting more angry, or taking a break from her) causes least damage to the relationship between myself and my child?' Separating from your child may cause them anxiety, may increase the likelihood of the screaming getting worse, but it may enable you to take a deep breath and regulate your own very challenging emotions. Trying to comfort your child at a time like this might work. It may calm them and make them feel that you are invested in them and want to understand their distress (it also might not, of course). Even if this does work, however, it may be that it has a negative impact on the relationship between you. It may be that you have not had an opportunity to regulate and you may feel more resentful and angrier at your child and more likely to carry that resentment into the rest of the day.

Each and every response to trauma-based challenging behaviour needs to be weighed up in this way: 'What is the best possible thing I can do for the relationship between me and my child?' Not just 'What do they need me to do?' or 'What do I need?' It requires a judgement call, which might mean having to do what you know is not in the best short-term interests of one or the other of you. The judgement call will best serve you and your child in the long term by preserving what is the most important thing in the world to them: their relationship with you (despite what they might say and make you feel!).

Prioritizing the relationship between you and your child may mean doing things that involve emotional acceptance, but also behavioural containment. For example, you may need to protect yourself from harm *and* from them developing an idea of themselves as a violent child who hurts the people who love them.

Reading beneath the behaviour

When you move from a reward–punishment approach towards emotional acceptance, it is useful to have a good idea of which emotions might be causing problematic behaviours and therefore which emotions we need to accept.

To help to clarify this for yourselves you could use an iceberg model. In EBM we are always seeking to intervene at the emotional level. All of that goes on below the water level. Intervening here enables us to develop a meaningful connection with our children that is based on understanding rather than judgement and a need to change. When we engage above the line (which we most certainly all will at some points), we simply recreate every negative relational pattern our children have ever known, and we can reinforce their sense that they are not good enough, perhaps faulty in some way, or not worthy of our understanding and compassion.

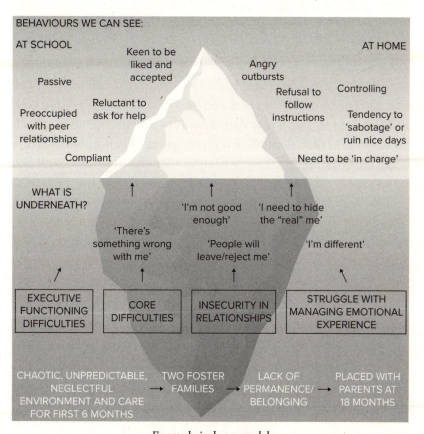

Example iceberg model
Source: With thanks to Dr Emmi Honeybourne-Ward for sharing this iceberg model

Empathic commentary

Empathic commentary has emotional acceptance at its core and so can be a useful tool in moving the focus away from behavioural change per se. For example:

- 'Oh wow! You pushed me. You're feeling so cross with me about something! There'll be a really good reason why you did that, but I just don't know what it is yet. I can't let you do that again, though.'
- 'Okay, I'm hearing that you're angry with Angie. Can I help to try and work out what's going on for you? You must be feeling awful about something.'

Adapting life

Sometimes, when behaviour change just isn't possible, there are adaptations to family life that can be made, although getting your head around this and reaching a point of acceptance about this is far easier said than done. Reaching the point of being able to accept behaviour that has previously been intolerable to you is tough and often simply takes time. It may require you to grieve for the type of family life you had anticipated and hoped for.

Sally Donovan[62, 63] talks of her struggle with her child's apparent need to squirt copious amounts of shower gel out in the shower each time they were in there. After battling over time and trying to change this behaviour, she eventually decided to assertively accept the behaviour and bought a job lot of very cheap shower gel that her child could squirt.

Reframing injustice

Often, it is a sense of injustice that drives our focus on behaviour change over emotional acceptance. That sense of injustice should be honoured. It is *not* fair that *anyone* has to cope with a life that is dominated by trauma, and parents and carers can feel like they are emotional punch bags for their children.

That injustice can take on a victim–perpetrator dynamic in parent–child relationships. The child is viewed as the unjust one and the parent as the victim (although those roles can be reversed). It can be useful, however, to reframe that very real injustice and direct it where it really belongs – to the trauma that hurt your child. I'd caution against redirecting it to the adults in your child's history (who may be perceived to have caused the trauma), as this has a knock-on effect for your child's sense of identity, and can imply that your child has an inherent 'badness' due to their connection with their birth family. The trauma can be characterized and given life via giving it a name, talking about 'the trauma/bad stuff/the hurting', etc., as a separate entity to you and your child. Maybe even drawing 'the trauma' with your child, writing letters to it, etc. This enables you to separate your child from their trauma in both your mind and that of your child. If you're interested in this idea, take a look at Chapter 4 of my previous book, *Why Can't My Child Behave?*

In naming this injustice, we create an understanding of both you, your child and anyone else impacted by this trauma-driven behaviour, as being victims of the injustice of abuse and/or neglect that has caused your child more suffering than anybody. In doing this you can unite against a common enemy and really think together about how to tackle 'the trauma' rather than both or all feeling at its mercy.

Preparing your network

Even when we've got our heads around approaching behaviour via emotional acceptance, it's tough to get the rest of the world to catch up. It's important to have this conversation with family and anyone else who may be having regular interactions with you and your child, which is particularly hard when we feel criticized for how we're parenting. The best we can do is, first, provide people with the right things to read; second, talk to them lots and hear their suspicions and concerns (easier said than done when you've got enough on your plate, I know), but be clear and assertive, and finally, work on developing a thick skin. Know that others may not get it straight away, and ignore the looks and comments you might get. After all, if the old, frankly easier stuff worked, why would you waste your time doing it the tough way?

Investing in emotional acceptance when faced with problem behaviour is not easy. It takes resilience and fortitude and we will all fail at times. It may, in fact, require a grieving process for the type of parent we thought we would be, indeed the type of family life we thought we would have. However, if we can allow ourselves to abandon the idea that we must, to be good parents, get our child to do everything we think they should be doing, it's so tremendously liberating, and it opens a whole new world of mutual interest and cooperation.

'FILLING UP' OR ACCEPTING DEPENDENCY NEEDS

Introduction

Attention-seeking, attachment-seeking, regressive behaviours, playing with younger children's toys, watching TV meant for younger children, clinginess – these are all behaviours that relate to a child's feelings of dependency on adults and indicate a child's need to connect with their younger self.

Therapeutic parenting can restart a healthy developmental process that may have stalled in your child's very early months or may have been set off course from the beginning. This chapter is about giving parents and carers confidence in that developmental process. To support it, we need to tune into a child's emotions and therefore their communications. We will then be able to read when a child is ready to move on from something they once needed, such as being walked to school, being cuddled to sleep, or using a dummy.

Trying to wean children off these things prematurely and according to our own agenda is likely to create greater shame, and is unlikely to be positive for their mental health.

So what is dependency and why does it happen? Dependency is more than any one of the things listed above, and it comes from a psychological and biological imperative. It is an essential stage of human development, arguably more than a stage, something that simply changes in intensity and direction as we mature. We always need other people, but we need them to different degrees and in different ways throughout our lives.

Humans, unlike other animals, are born entirely biologically dependent on other, adult humans. We cannot feed ourselves or protect ourselves from danger; we are just not able to keep ourselves alive without dependence on someone who will do those things for us. We are also psychologically and neurologically dependent. Our brains do not develop to their full potential unless we have the sensitive, devoted care of an adult. The one skill that baby humans are most certainly born with is the ability to make themselves as hard to ignore, and as compelling to pay attention to, as possible. This survival skill is played out when dependency becomes a tricky issue between parents and carers and older children.

Typically, through experience of sensitive, attuned care, babies grow into toddlers who can venture further from their primary carer to explore their world. They then develop into children who can separate and come back together with their grown-ups confidently and without prolonged distress. Without early care that meets a child's need for touch, proximity and emotional understanding, the needs must be muted, or they quite simply remain. It is a developmental process for which there is no shortcut.

Unfortunately, when those needs are not met in a child's early months and years, it is not as simple as just making up for lost time later. There is a critical period for developing attachment security and therefore the ability to feel confident away from one's carer. After such time, attachment security can be improved but it takes much more time, energy and patience.

Put simply, in order to foster independence in children, we must first encourage and embrace dependence, regardless of how old a child is and what our age-based expectations of them might be.

What do we mean by 'weaning off'?

Behaviour we might try to wean children off:

- Watching CBeebies, when it might seem they're too old, based on their chronological age.

- Using a dummy at night.
- Sucking their thumb.
- Needing you to sit with them at night until they go to sleep.
- Talking with a baby voice.
- Wanting you to clean their teeth for them.
- Wanting you to read to them rather than them reading for themselves.
- Always wanting to be in the same room as you.

If your child is displaying any of the behaviours listed above, but you would not typically expect the behaviour for their age, it may be that they are feeling more vulnerable in their aloneness and more dependent on you than their peers are on their parents or carers.

Using a traditional reward–punishment approach, we may well be drawn towards trying to stop those behaviours as they may be seen as undesirable, not age-appropriate, embarrassing for the child, triggering for adults, or just downright annoying and exhausting!

As a result, parents may fall into rewarding independent behaviour and setting consequences for dependent behaviour, even though these strategies may shame what is an unmet emotional need. The traditional approach can force children to mask an inner world that they cannot change. In other words, they may occasionally, when stress is low, be able to inhibit their need to be close to you or avoid reaching for their dummy to regulate their emotions. Ultimately, however, if their behaviour is due to an unmet need, the cost to them of inhibiting their need to be close to you or behaving in 'babyish' ways may be feelings of loneliness, not belonging, fear or dysregulation. This is made worse by the isolation that comes from not being able to share these feelings with you. If your child did share, they would then be confronted by the shame that you might judge their inner world as bad or repellent in some way.

What do we mean by 'filling up'?

A therapeutic parenting approach to dependency would be to focus on 'filling up' or exhausting a child's need for dependence rather than 'weaning them off' it. This is based on the developmental understanding that children start with the need to be close to their adult for their survival; also that given the right support, children develop the trust and confidence to explore their environment and to venture further away from their secure base when they are safe and confident to do so. Dependence comes before (healthy) independence.

Taking this 'filling up' approach requires us to overcome the impulses to push children away when they take more attention than feels fair, appropriate and/or comfortable. It also means we need to resist the pulls to make sure our children are keeping up with their peers' developmental progress. The solution is to pull closer rather than push away, to trust our child's instincts rather than a chronological timetable. That's not to say that this is easy or even possible *every* time.

To use this empathic approach, we also need to be attuned to our children's signals about when they need us and how much independence they can tolerate. As with all therapeutic parenting strategies, we never just rest on our laurels or stick with one position. As children change and grow, so does our parenting. However, the difference is that we need to be more attuned to what our child's behaviour is telling us. We can decide on the timetable based on what their cues tell us and notice the right developmental time for small steps towards areas of independence. Attunement empowers us to see things we otherwise wouldn't; it gives us a sensitive barometer of when our children are ready to try a little bit of extra independence. This is often referred to as the 'window of tolerance' (see below).[64] We only know whether children have developed enough to move away a little or into slightly more 'grown-up' activities when they show us, or we test what they are capable of.

If we use the more traditional parenting approach (trying to wean a child off their dependency), when that dependency is driven by unmet emotional needs or an innate (constitutional) vulnerability (anxiety, nervousness, a disability or autistic traits), it is highly likely that the dependency behaviour will actually increase rather than decrease. This is because pushing a child into independence, for which they are not ready, will increase the child's anxiety (particularly separation anxiety) and create a rebound effect. This means they will cling on for dear life to you (or *CBeebies*, baby toys, their dummy – all the things they use to deal with their anxiety) rather than feeling more confident or more persuaded that they can safely move away.

✸ SOPHIE, SAM AND HARVEY

Sophie is a 7-year-old girl who lives with her adoptive parents, Sam and Harvey. She has lived with them since she was 2 years old. Sophie has always been closest to her adoptive mum, Sam, and is reluctant to let her mum out of her sight. The family is typically a calm and happy one, but they have started to fall out about toothbrushing. Sophie will brush her teeth but often refuses to do so unless Sam sits in the bathroom with her. Sophie says that without Sam there she feels too scared. She will scream and cry and refuse to brush her teeth, simply following Sam around the house rather than risk being alone. Sophie's reaction to toothbrushing time is more extreme if she is tired or having a tough time in some way. The fact that Sophie will occasionally do her teeth without too much protest makes Sam and Harvey think that her protests aren't sincere and that she is 'attention-seeking'.

Reality: the exhausted Hare	Traditional: 'weaning off' dependency	Therapeutic: 'filling up' dependency needs
✗	✗	✓
(Unpredictable)	(Not trauma-informed)	(Trauma-informed)

Comparison of approaches

Reality: the exhausted Hare
Approach

Before we start to think about what the traditional and then the therapeutic (EBM) approach would encourage us to do in response to Sophie, let's explore what our instinctive, impulsive Hare system might lead us to do. This is a somewhat typical response that all of us can get to when we've lived with challenging and/or frustrating behaviour for long enough. It's not necessarily an ideal response, but it is a reasonably typical one.

Techniques

Sam generally does okay with Sophie's need to be close to her, but she gets very frustrated when Sophie won't brush her teeth without her being with her as time is tight in the mornings and Sam needs to get herself and Sophie's little sister ready to go out too.

Sam generally starts fairly patiently with Sophie and will tell her calmly that it is time to brush her teeth. Usually, this triggers angry, upset shouting and screaming from Sophie: 'BUT I'M SCARED!'

Sam will vary between trying to reassure Sophie from another room whilst she gets on with getting herself and her other daughter dressed – 'It's okay, Soph, I'm right here but we're in a hurry now, so please just get your teeth brushed' – and getting cross – 'Sophie, will you just do your teeth! I've got to get your sister ready and myself! I can't just drop everything and sit with you! The world doesn't revolve around you, Sophie!'

Traditional: 'weaning off' dependency (reward–punishment)

Approach

A reward–punishment approach would encourage Sam and Harvey to steel themselves, exercise self-discipline, stay calm and resist shouting at Sophie. The approach would focus on discouraging the behaviour Sam and Harvey don't like, that is, the 'tantrums or attention-seeking' or screaming and shouting, and encouraging more positive behaviour – Sophie brushing her teeth without protest.

There may be space in this approach to give Sophie a chance to discuss her fears about being alone, but this would be separate from discouraging the problematic behaviours.

Techniques

Sam and Harvey may be encouraged to try one or a few of the following:

- They could try a progressive step-by-step programme that gradually moves towards Sophie brushing her teeth alone. This would start with being present in the bathroom and moving away in small increments day by day (according to a set programme rather than in response to Sophie's apparent confidence).
- They may give Sophie a sticker on a chart for achieving the goal for each day, for example, tolerating Sam standing outside the bathroom rather than being right beside her.
- They may choose to ignore the angry behaviour from Sophie, not talking to her or responding to her protests.
- Sam and Harvey might praise Sophie if she managed to do her teeth a little more independently than the day before.

Therapeutic: 'filling up' dependency needs (EBM)
Approach

An EBM approach to dependency needs would mean Sam and Harvey both taking time for themselves to understand how Sophie's behaviour impacts on them. They could explore how it makes them feel and what it might trigger for them from their past. They could then use this understanding to be kind to themselves and each other when they get frustrated or downright angry with Sophie. Only then could they move on to starting to think about how to approach the toothbrushing issues differently with Sophie.

Using EBM, Sam and Harvey would refocus on trusting Sophie's cues. They would do so with an acceptance that her cues may absolutely be about attention or attachment-seeking, but that they need to be understood too, and there may well be an attention need to be met before it will disappear. They would be helped to think about the developmental effect of encouraging dependence in order to foster independence. However, the EBM approach will not produce fast results with something like this. In this instance, EBM is simply facilitating an automatic developmental process rather than fighting against it.

Techniques

- Toothbrushing time can be approached as a connecting, nurturing time. The adoptive parents could offer to do Sophie's teeth for her until she feels ready to move on to the next step, then reading her cues and using them to determine when she might be ready to move to the next stage; for example, the parents do a minute and Sophie does a minute. This, of course, takes a little bit of planning and may necessitate getting the family up a bit earlier so everyone can still be ready on time. Settling in and accepting the dependence rather than seeing it as a means to an end is important here.

- Another way is to make a game of giving Sophie a solid five-minute cuddle before toothbrushing time, preparing her for toothbrushing time.

- Sam and Harvey may also try a progressive effort to encourage Sophie's confidence whilst brushing her teeth. Sophie would only move on to the next stage when she was happy and able to do so, when each step had increased her confidence. This might start with a parent being present in the bathroom and then moving away in small increments. This may take a long time, perhaps months spent on one step before the next step is tried. There may also be steps backwards during this time and they wouldn't be resisted. This progressive, child-led process would be responsive to Sophie's mood and capacity on any given day.

Let's get practical
Separating what we're doing for ourselves from what we're doing for our children

This is one of the first and most powerful mental exercises you can do for both you and your child. Parenting is at its most confusing and distressing when we act in ways we wish we hadn't, without knowing why. Our impulses (Hare system decisions) take over so often in parenting that we need to work out where those impulses come from. One very powerful place such impulses come from is our own experience of being parented, as we have explored in previous chapters. The other key (linked) factor is a powerful drive to meet our own psychological needs. The good news is that this is no bad thing – as long as we know whose need is being met and we're honest with ourselves and our children about it. So often, we put in place a rule, sanction or boundary for our children 'because *they* need it', when really it is *us* who needs it. Putting such things in place is absolutely fine, but doing so without knowledge of why can leave us open to disconnection with our children and separation from an awareness of our own needs and welfare.

Let's consider some examples: first, stopping your child from watching the same TV programme that they've watched three times already this week; and second, ensuring they come home from their friend's house at 5pm. Both of these things could absolutely be for their benefit, but in different circumstances they might be for your benefit. In the first example, you may consider that it's not very stimulating for your child to watch the same TV programme again. Alternatively, you may be bored to tears by hearing the same TV theme tune for the umpteenth time that week. In the second example, parents might want to make sure their child is home to do homework, but it may, in fact, not do a particular child any harm at all to be out later than 5pm on one occasion. Parents' motivation to get their children home may be more about a desire to spend time with them or a need to feel in control. All of those motivations are entirely understandable and good reasons for putting in place a boundary. What gets confusing, however, is when we try to falsely convince our children and ourselves that the boundary is for their benefit rather than for our own.

In relation to 'weaning off' vs. 'filling up' dependency needs, this comes up a great deal, as it is hugely demanding to try and exhaust the dependency needs of a child who has not had their relational needs met in their early months and years. Examples in this context might be ignoring a child's cries when they scream disproportionately after they've bumped their knee, or insisting that a child stay in their room at night rather than come to you because 'they're too old to be doing that'. An understanding of these as developmental needs that cannot be shortcut but must be worked through tells us that any attempt to discipline our child into this is doomed to fail and is unhelpful for their emotional wellbeing. However, many of us still do it and tell the story as though it's for our child's benefit to help them learn or be more disciplined.

So why do we still try to coach our children through things that are unmet developmental needs, even if sometimes we know we cannot 'train' this discipline into them? It is often done because we can't tolerate any more interaction, any more need. With children who need more from us than we expect at a given age, we can become drained very easily and do some mental gymnastics (often unconsciously) to free us from the guilt and shame of our need to push them away. In order to free ourselves from that guilt and shame, we change the story in our heads. Rather than 'I can't bear my child being near me right now', we change it to 'They need to do this themselves for their own benefit'.

The biggest problem with this strategy, although it can help us to feel better, is that it transfers the shame from us to them. Children then become responsible for being pushed away: 'If only they could manage this by themselves, I wouldn't have to push them away.' Or, from a child's perspective: 'If I wasn't so needy my mum wouldn't be so disappointed in me.' Children might try to do what is asked of them, but if they are not developmentally ready to do so, they will inevitably fail and feel the shame of being inadequate and insufficient (that is, they are not up to the task asked of them, they are not enough, unconsciously, in the eyes of their parents).

When our needs and those of our child conflict (for example, a child needs to be close while their parent needs time alone), we often decide to override our own needs, particularly when they are less of a priority than our child's and it feels doable, such as knowing you'll miss a TV show to read them that extra story. At other times, the best we can do is help our child to make sense of our inability to meet their need. What can be *unhelpful* is rewriting reality to try and tell them that those needs don't exist or that we are meeting them when we're not.

There is, however, a wonderful alternative! It requires a lot of reflective capacity and self-acceptance from parents, but in essence it's simple. When we need to apply a boundary to our child's access to us or to the way they conduct their relationship with us, such as physical or relational proximity, we can simply own the problem!

Empathic commentary

Discussing your child's needs and your own in an honest, straightforward way can provide an excellent way of modelling how all of our needs can be accepted and nurtured. For example, when adult capacity to be empathic to a child's needs for more and more attention is low, you can try any of the following:

- 'I know you really want to sit right up close to me today, but I'm feeling like I need to be in my own bubble for a little while. I'm so sorry, I'll be back to being squeezed up close as soon as I possibly can!'
- 'I struggle so much with being woken up in the night; it makes me really grumpy with you, doesn't it? I know you only wake me up because you're scared and lonely and I wish I could be less grumpy. I'm so sorry. I don't want you to have to feel scared on your own, though, so we'll make sure Daddy comes to you because he doesn't get as many grumpy feelings when he's tired as I do.'
- 'I know it's a struggle for you when I'm not here and it makes you grumpy with me when I come home. I do have to have some time to myself, though; that's not because of you, it's because I'm just a person who likes a lot of my own time and you're someone who likes to be close to the people they love. Neither one is wrong! We're just going to have to work it out so we both get what we need.'

Zones of regulation

To manage the relative priorities of our needs and those of our child, having a system in place can help. 'Zones of regulation'[65] is one such system. Much like the traffic light system in my previous book, *Why Can't My Child Behave?*, it helps parents and children communicate about their internal world and the degree of need at any given time.

This won't be news to any of you, but often children who have experienced early trauma don't have a way of communicating about their inner world, particularly about the variations and gradations of need at any given time. Practising and trying out talking with your child about their experiences and your own in terms of the zones of regulation can help to build this skill. You can start by noticing states and emotions at home and labelling them in terms of the zones: blue, green, yellow or red.

Zones of regulation

Blue zone	Sad, 'poorly', bored, tired, 'down' emotions
Green zone	Neutral emotions, organized cognitive and emotional states: calm, happy, focused, okay
Yellow zone	Heightened emotions, but with cognitive control: annoyed, frustrated, silly, excited, agitated, overwhelmed, giggly, nervous
Red zone	Intense emotions that overwhelm: rageful, panicking, over-excited, elated, screaming, sobbing

Once you understand the zone that you and your child are in at any given time, you can tailor your response. If your child is in the red zone, there's no doubt about it – they need you. That might mean you will have to regulate your own need and respond entirely how your child needs you to. However, the reality is that you might not be able to do this. If you are in the red zone yourself, it may be too difficult to prioritize your child's need. In this case the best you can do is comment on that fact and help your child not to feel the shame of that disconnection whilst you take care of yourself. This will also need repair when things are calmer.

In the blue zone, your child will most certainly have a high level of need, but they may not necessarily make demands of you; they may become quieter or more withdrawn. These are the times when gentle proactive action, such as sitting with your child and being curious about their inner world, can be very powerful, but also very challenging. Making yourself overtly available to a child who is withdrawn and distant can be a challenge; it can feel rejecting and dismissive, so keep an eye on what zone you are in, too.

When your child is in the green zone, they are likely to have more ability to regulate themselves and can often wait for a need to be met.

In the yellow zone, when they have needs but also have more cognitive control, you may have to make a judgement call about whose needs to prioritize (evaluate which zone you yourself are in). In the yellow zone your child will have some tolerance, but only so much.

The 'window of tolerance'

The 'window of tolerance'[66] is another way in which we can judge just how much dependency your child has and how much independence they can tolerate.

The 'window of tolerance' also helps us to address the myth that sometimes comes up about therapeutic parenting and attachment-informed parenting: that it is somehow permissive and anti-aspirational. Therapeutic parenting certainly does have room within it for change by gently pushing children's comfort zones. However, change happens via attunement and understanding what is possible for a child at a given time rather than via chronological age expectations or because of some other agenda that is outside of the child themselves.

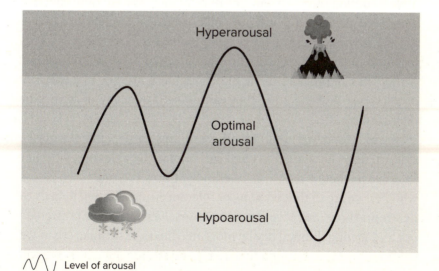

The window of tolerance

The window of tolerance is that calm, receptive state in which we are able to learn, develop and have positive relationships. Above this window is 'hyperarousal', where feelings are large, loud and uncontained. A person in this state may look angry, over-excited and/or dysregulated. Underneath the window of tolerance is 'hypoarousal', when we can be shut down, unresponsive or withdrawn. A person in this state might look sad, depressed or feel numb and absent. These states are linked with arousal in our brains and the ways in which these areas function under stress.

These states are perfectly normal and functional, but there is only one optimal state in which humans can fully explore their world and relationships and get the most from life. Often, for children impacted by early abuse and/or trauma, their window of tolerance will be smaller than that of someone who hasn't had this experience. The size of that window can only be changed from within – at the start we need to meet children where they are and accept what they say they can do. We have to wait for times when our children are calm and responsive before we can hope to push their comfort zones a little and stretch their window of tolerance.

Change for traumatized children depends on relationships with their primary carers. Therefore, another key element to this is understanding our own window of tolerance. We are only effective in our communication and our ability to teach and learn when we are in our window of tolerance (or as close to it as we can get!). This is why shouting or criticizing from a place of dysregulation never works. Our brains and those of our children are not in a window of tolerance, and therefore they cannot be productive in actions or relationships.

So, in relation to 'weaning off' vs. 'filling up' dependency needs, we can judge how much a child can tolerate by assessing whether they are in their window of tolerance or not. We must also assess whether we are in that window of tolerance, and this will help us to determine how much we can give of ourselves. When we're stressed out and feeling drained dry by more neediness or intimacy than we can handle, it is not a good time to try and stretch ourselves. We will inevitably spring to hyper-or hypoarousal, becoming snappy, irritated and angry or shut down, dismissive or even rejecting. Trying to do more than we are able to will lead to far more damage to our children, ourselves and our relationship than a calm acknowledgement (using empathic commentary, see above) that you do not have capacity right now. Acknowledging and highlighting when we cannot do what is optimal is far more effective and supportive than disciplining oneself and pushing hard to do what is 'right', potentially giving a dysregulated response instead.

In response to the things we hear or even say, like 'They need to get used to the real world' or 'Other people won't mollycoddle them like that', we need to accept that 'real-world' expectations do not and cannot shape the 'internal world' of children who have experienced early trauma. What you can do, however, is hear what your child is feeling whilst simultaneously still respecting what, unfortunately, has to be done. This may either be due to immovable external expectations or due to our own limited capacity. What won't change, however, is what is right for your child.

Sometimes when faced with a dependency need, we are able to focus on trying to accept or 'fill it'. However, at other times we have to act based on our own capacity or external demands, whilst knowing it is not optimal for our child and that it might, in fact, temporarily decrease their feelings of security (which we can work to repair later). Sometimes in these cases the best we can do is mediate during and repair afterwards.

BUILDING MOTIVATION AND HOPE

Introduction

A new computer game, an extra hour of TV, stickers on a sticker chart – these are all examples of the rewards parents frequently use to help manage the behaviour and safety of their children. As with all matters in EBM, our concern is twofold. Does it work, and does it help your child to grow beyond their trauma? I think most of us find rewards helpful at times – they work, right? At least sometimes. In assessing whether they are good for children's emotional wellbeing we need to consider why we reward, how we reward and, most importantly, what impact the reward has on your relationship with your child.

Sometimes, when parents and carers come to people like me for help, it is not huge disastrous behaviours that are damaging family relationships but a relentless lack of cooperation or the struggle of not being able to get a child to do what needs to be done – putting clothes in the laundry basket, cleaning teeth, eating meals, getting up for school, etc.

Exploration of rewards
Why do we reward?

Parents generally use rewards to encourage their children to behave in the way they want them to – to do their homework, to tidy their rooms, etc. Usually when we look at it through the lens of traditional parenting, we see rewards as a way to control our children's behaviour in order to get them to do what we need or want them to do. Often, of course, this is for the child's benefit – to help them learn at school, to guide them towards being a positive part of the family, or to encourage them to engage in behaviours that will be healthy for them. However, when we look at rewards in this traditional way, we can't help but see it as a thing we are doing to our child – *we* are in control of the reward and *they* need to meet our criteria. This way of wielding control can be a trigger for many developmentally traumatized children (but I don't need to tell you that!).

How do we reward?

Generally, when it comes to 'rewarding' behaviour, we take charge and we are in a position of control. The narrative is something like 'Tidy your room and then you can have a chocolate bar later'. It's very much framed as something an adult is doing to a child and the child is the subject. This is not necessarily a problem, but it is necessarily disconnecting and therefore often triggering for a child who has experienced early trauma. This approach disconnects, because it's a sledgehammer of a reminder to your child that someone else has power over them. In the past, their formative experience of power has been an abusive one. It is 'triggering' because when children are connected with the idea of abusive power, they will be thrown back, emotionally and neurologically, to react against the threat of that abuse of power.

There is an additional problem in using rewards. As with all traditional parenting strategies, it encourages us away from understanding 'why?'. When we implement a reward 'system' to get our children to do the things we need (or want) them to do, we are instantly discouraged from exploring why this thing is difficult to achieve, agree with or engage with. What is it that makes a child not want to get their school bag ready for the morning? Or not have a shower? Our gut reaction in response to this is maybe 'Why would they want to do it, unless we make not doing it hard for them in some way?' Well, that's an understandable question, but it comes from our experience of the same sorts of approaches, of being disciplined into doing things we don't want to do. What if there was another way? A shift in focus to making the thing a desirable activity, something that is not just attached to a reward but something that feels more intrinsically rewarding.

I know this all sounds like pretty harmless stuff, but my point is only to offer a slant on the strategy that might just be more effective and create a better connection.

If the thing we are trying to change is a trauma-driven behaviour, rewards are very unlikely to help. We cannot persuade a child to give up a strategy that has helped them survive their trauma or one that is so driven by impulse that they have no conscious, deliberate control over it.

However, there are times, for children traumatized by abuse, just like any child, when some task or another feels too much. Particularly for traumatized children, cooperating with what adults want just might feel impossible. It may be that a developmentally traumatized child's need to stay in control (which is the best way of staying safe) overrides any desire to accept the parent's guidance or to please that parent.

What impact do rewards have?

For many non-traumatized brains (and, in fact, many traumatized ones) it's tough to imagine anything other than the positives of a reward, the anticipation and joy of success, the positive aspiration and the buzz that entails. However, for many developmentally traumatized children the element of reward that looms largest is the prospect of failure leading to loss, disapproval and self-criticism. When shame and disconnection are what you expect as the default, the potential of reward is just another negative experience. This is why so many traumatized children react badly to them (including praise used as a reward).

There are slight adjustments we can make in our thinking and in our approach to rewards that can make them a positive, connecting experience for you and your child.

Building motivation

Sometimes the reality of raising children is that we need them to do things – often mundane, everyday things. We need them to wash, stop watching TV, do the washing-up, etc. When there is resistance from our children to doing these things, it's important to establish the reasons why a task is so aversive or unappealing.

Much of the resistance to cooperation with developmentally traumatized children can be in the dynamic it causes between parents or carers and their children: 'I'm being made to do something'. It's a very obvious sign that a child's control is being taken away. Another reason can be that a child or young person 'can't be bothered'. Although this sounds like a simple dead end, there is still value in exploring 'why?' Why can't they be bothered? Take a moment and think about the thing your child is most interested in: football, Minecraft, cooking, texting friends, posting on social media. They are motivated then; they don't need you to pester, cajole and reward those things into being (quite the opposite, I'm sure!). Maybe we can tap into some of that motivation. It may also be that using a reward when motivation is low is a good way to increase motivation. So why bother with critiquing this process and coming up with an empathy-based alternative? If rewards can be therapeutic, why don't we just skip all this and use them? Well, as with a fair few of the traditional parenting strategies, they may well still be helpful, but they benefit from a different approach. Approaching the same strategy from a different angle can most definitely produce a different effect. It's like looking through the same glasses but with different lenses in – it gives you different options. When using an empathic approach, we get a better understanding of what our children are really experiencing and thus a more precise tool with which to motivate them differently.

Why build motivation?

Why focus on motivation rather than achievement and success? With most things therapeutic, this is more about the process than the outcome. First, it means we can get around the difficulties that many developmentally traumatized children have with imagining the future, investing in something that they can't yet feel or benefit from. Second, talking about what will help this to feel easier and more achievable is a way of levelling the conversation; it takes away the disconnecting power dynamic between adult and child. Building an alliance with your child in achieving a goal is inherently more motivating and inspiring for a child who has previously had abusive experiences of power held over them. Third, focusing on the process of how your child is experiencing motivation about a given task makes it less of an evaluative experience, and therefore they will experience less judgement and anticipation of failure and shame.

If talk of levelling the power imbalance starts to give you the jitters, it may be worth looking back at Superpower #2: Safe Containment, which fully explores the need for parental control but talks in terms of having control *for* rather than control *of*.

How do we build motivation?

How do we use rewards in a motivational-focused way? We need to adjust our focus from *doing to* to *doing with*. The key to this, as with so many other elements of therapeutic parenting, is communication. When using rewards, we typically start with a problem behaviour and work out a strategy to apply to solve that problem. When we approach rewards from an empathic point of view, we start with questions, wonderings: 'I wonder why this is hard for you?', 'What can I do to help?', 'Can you think of anything that would make it easier?'

It is possible through this process and using some empathic commentary (see 'Let's get practical' below) that you are able to come to a shared understanding of why completing a task is difficult or feels unsatisfying for the child. This can be unrelated to developmental trauma (for example, 'I hate doing maths') or about a conflict-based way of relating, which may be due to trauma, (for example, 'I hate it when you tell me what to do'). The subtext of the latter, that you might come up with and talk about together, could be related to a struggle with trust and an experience of parental relationships as abusive.

You can also extend the conversation to develop your understanding of the unpredictable consequences of struggling with doing what they need to do; for example, 'How does it feel when we fall out over you cleaning your teeth?' or 'What was it like when your teacher told you off for not doing your homework?' We might sometimes ask these questions when approaching from a traditional parenting perspective, but this would typically be an attempt to get a child to realize the 'error' of their ways. Asking with empathy and a genuine desire to understand what this is like for a child can mean your child has a powerful experience of feeling understood. This will bring you closer together and give you all the information you need to take the next steps towards helping them.

The next stage would be to be curious with your child about what might help get their teeth cleaned without it bringing up all the feelings and challenges that they've explained to you: 'Any ideas on how we can fix this without you feeling like I'm controlling you? Because I know that's really difficult for you – no wonder, given what you've been through!'

If, through these conversations, you work out between you that some external motivation, like a sticker or a cake or a trip out at the weekend, would feel more like a victory than a loss, like a success more than a failure, like a beacon of realistic hope, like a shared celebration rather than a point of conflict, then rewards are great! Use them, celebrate them, enjoy them. Use them to connect and share joy with your child! *But*, be prepared for the fact that they might not bring the joy that you both hope for. And if they don't, you can just try something else.

Why build hope?

In this context, motivation and hope are fundamentally interlinked. All of the above also applies to building hope, but there is an added heart-swelling, awe-inspiring dimension. If we don't have hope, then how could any of us possibly bother to try with anything? Any investment in ourselves, in our relationships, in the world at large would be pointless, but more crucially, it would simply be impossible.

Typically, when developmentally traumatized children and young people are doing something (or not doing something) for which we might reach for rewards, they have little hope that they can be different, that their relationship with you can be different, that the world can be different. After all, if there was hope, then a reward might just work, but time and time again we see what little effect rewards actually have on our children.

A reward is typically enough of an incentive to get you past just not being bothered, but it is most certainly *not* enough to bring you hope at a time of hopelessness. Imagine, for example, you were hungry and had nothing to eat. Also imagine that someone more powerful than you said that they would buy you a meal if you could jump over the nearest house. What would your internal and external reactions be? You'd instantly feel despondent. You might feel shame that someone thinks you should be able to do something that you know is impossible. You'd also probably feel rageful and disgusted with the person who dangled something you desperately needed but without a realistic chance of success. It's the heart breaking equivalent of asking a child to do something they just can't bring themselves to do. Unfortunately, it happens all too often in relation to children's behaviour. Many times, I have seen children, in foster or residential care, told that if they improve their behaviour, they'll be able to go home to their parents or have contact with them. Whilst this isn't often a formal strategy and is mostly borne out of frustration, it is a reality many children are confronted with. Although our efforts to change behaviour with a reward may seem in a very different league, sometimes they're really not.

The point is we *cannot* know how difficult something is to change or how important a reward is for our children until we trust their resistance and really get to know why change is difficult for them.

How do we build hope?

Building hope and building motivation come via the same process. All of the above applies here too. Put simply, we shift from *doing to* to *doing with*. This means trusting that your child's resistance to change comes from a sensible place, and then doing your damnedest to understand it. The techniques below will help in the nuts and bolts of how to build hope.

✳ AMAIRA, SOBIA AND ARJUN

Amaira is 14 and lives with her foster carers, Sobia and Arjun. She has lived with them for the past 10 years. Generally, the family is settled and there is lots of love. Sobia, however, is struggling in her relationship with Amaira. She finds herself 'constantly' getting really frustrated with Amaira. She says that Amaira won't do anything she's asked to do, 'literally anything'. Sobia says the mornings and evenings are always a battle ground in the home. She feels frustrated because she has to nag, cajole and ultimately force Amaira to brush her teeth, shower, get dressed – basically anything that needs to happen before the family can get out in the mornings or get to bed. Amaira will avoid all of those tasks, and Sobia will find her looking at her phone in bed or generally doing anything but what needs to be done.

Reality: the exhausted Hare	Traditional: rewards	Therapeutic: building motivation and hope
✗	✗	✓
(Unpredictable)	(Not trauma-informed)	(Trauma-informed)

Comparison of approaches

Reality: the exhausted Hare
Approach

Before we start to think about what traditional and then therapeutic (EBM) approaches would encourage us to do in response to Amaira and Sobia, let's explore what our instinctive, impulsive Hare system might lead us to do. This is a somewhat typical response that all of us can get to when we've lived with challenging or frustrating behaviour for long enough. It's not necessarily an ideal response, but it is a reasonably typical one.

Techniques

Sobia says that most days she starts off relatively patient, but after three or four attempts to calmly encourage and motivate Amaira, she becomes snappy and critical: 'What is going on, Amaira? Why are you *still* not dressed? For goodness sake! I have to tell you this every day! Just get dressed and get downstairs! What is wrong with you?!' Amaira will often not react at all, or sometimes gets upset and then collapses in an emotional heap on her bed.

Traditional: rewards (reward–punishment)
Approach
If Sobia and Arjun were to take a traditional reward-based approach to the family's morning struggles, they might sit down, either just the two of them, or possibly with Amaira too, and plan out what desired responses they would like to see from Amaira, how they would make them achievable and what rewards they might give Amaira if or when she does achieve them.

Techniques
The family would spend time together talking about why not getting things done in the morning is difficult and what Amaira would really like to have as her (smaller) daily and then (larger) weekly rewards. They decide on an ink stamp (of Amaira's favourite boy band) on a chart each time she cleans her teeth, gets dressed or gets downstairs by 8am. They also decide that in the first week she can have a trip to the cinema if she gets at least 7 out of 21 stamps in a week (based on three stamps available per day, when one a day on average may be considered success). They all agree this is achievable.

Therapeutic: building motivation and hope (EBM)
Approach
The overarching principle when taking an empathic 'building motivation and hope' approach to this kind of challenge is to connect with your child and understand what is going on. This requires us to first be regulated enough to be empathic even when it impacts us negatively too, so timing and self-reflection are crucial. Striking when the iron is cold[67] can be a very useful approach when there is conflict around.

It's crucial that we view the problem as primarily a relational one rather than a problem that exists in Amaira alone. This means that we can own how difficult the situation is for us and in a contained way use that as part of the discussion with our child: 'I know I get really angry and I'm so sorry because I know it upsets you such a lot. I just can't change that part of me that gets frustrated and angry about it, though; it really presses my buttons. Can we try to find a better way because this way is no good for either of us?'

When everyone concerned is in a calm, empathic place, it may be possible to begin to think of practical solutions and find a hopeful and enthusiastic way out of the problem. This might involve specific rewards if you and your child genuinely think they inspire hope, are achievable and motivational for all.

Techniques

Step one: Sobia and Arjun would find their own support to vent, offload and feel understood in their reactions to Amaira, without feeling pressured by someone else's reaction or agenda (this is true of any and every EBM and therapeutic parenting technique!). The goal of this is to release Sobia and Arjun from any shame they may be feeling and any defensive blaming of Amaira (or anyone else). It may be necessary through this or a therapeutic consultation to find out why this process presses buttons to the degree it does. It may be that it triggers something in parents from their own parenting history.

Step two: the priority, for carers in Sobia and Arjun's situation, would be to connect with Amaira and talk with her about how the morning fall-outs make Amaira feel. What are they like for her? How do the foster carers' reactions make Amaira feel? This does not necessarily mean any individual taking blame or responsibility; it means positioning their relationship with Amaira at the heart of the discussion and as the casualty of these fall-outs. Ask 'How does it feel for you [and reflecting, in a contained way, about how it feels for you as the adult] when we argue and fall out in the mornings?' Showing genuine concern, interest and care for how this feels for Amaira at these times will help her reconnect, feel free (enough) of shame and offer the potential that she may be able to join her carers in a later stage of problem-solving.

Step three: if, and only if, steps one and two are successful and it seems that problem-solving will lead to greater connection, hope and motivation in the family, it may well be useful to move on to a problem-solving stage that *might* include rewards. In this eventuality it would feel exciting, inspiring and liberating to think of achievable ways of creating motivation for Amaira and her carers to do something different. They may decide to trial a reward-based approach that would require effort and change from both Amaira and her foster carers.

This may work in a similar way to that described in the rewards techniques section above, but discussions would have an emphasis on collaboration (as in the case of a traditional approach too). However, there will be less emphasis on lone, individual responsibility (and thus shame). There will be less language of 'trying hard', 'good behaviour' and 'effort', and more talk of 'trust' and 'I'll help you and you help me'.

Let's get practical
Self-reflective space
Because of the potential similarity between a traditional use of rewards and using them to build hope and motivation, it is VERY important that the adults using these techniques understand the big, but nuanced, difference. The invitation to use rewards in a heavy-handed, top-down way can be driven by (the wholly understandable) emotional reactions and expectations based on traditional reward–punishment thinking (which will come from our own experience of being parented too). If those emotions drive the tone of interactions, the technique will certainly and inevitably turn into a traditional approach, which is likely to increase shame and decrease connection.

Empathic commentary
Another way of emphasizing the difference in our approach in using motivational and hope-building rewards is to commentate on what

we imagine to be going on for our child in an empathic way. You can also commentate on what is going on in the relationship between you and your child. This has the effect of normalizing emotional reactions (both yours and theirs), reducing shame and connecting you on equal terms.

Using empathic commentary, we can help our children to understand that we understand why these things are difficult and that we want to help, rather than blame. We can communicate that whilst we can't take the challenge away, we can face it *with* our child.

Empathic commentary for building motivation and hope includes:

- 'I know getting homework done is feeling hard. I want to try and help and not be so grumpy if I can.'
- 'I'm so sorry we keep falling out about you getting showered. I find myself getting so frustrated and annoyed about it, but then I can see that this makes you angry, and I'm guessing you feel like I'm trying to control you.'
- 'I wonder why we're struggling with this so much at the moment?! It's so hard to find the motivation to get going, isn't it? I wonder if I can help in some way? What do you think?'
- 'It's so hard for you to leave your phone downstairs at night-time isn't it? Something feels really good about having it with you and being able to chat to your friends whenever they're available. I'm sorry I have to step in when you don't want me to. Can you help me understand why it's so important?'
- 'We've been arguing about you emptying the dishwasher each morning for what seems like forever – that's no good for us, is it?! You've started to look so sad about it, as well as annoyed. It's like you've lost all hope that we can sort this problem out and we'll just keep falling out! Maybe we need something that's going to make this feel achievable! I've got some ideas, if you're interested?'

Change from personal discipline to interactive motivation

Getting this right is really just a matter of getting into the right groove, but it can feel like quite a huge shift for some. You can start by placing your focus on the language of the two different mindsets. Discipline is a solo endeavour that we associate with willpower, whereas motivation can be a more collaborative process that you, as parents and carers, can be involved in, in a supportive and positive way. 'Failures of discipline' can easily bring shame and blame, whereas 'struggles with motivation' can encourage joint strategizing about what you and your child can do together to build the desire for, and positivity of, success.

In practical terms, then, try if you can (with yourself and with your children), to build your language in these areas around the words in the interactive motivation column rather than the personal discipline column in the table below.

Personal discipline and interactive motivational language

Personal discipline	Interactive motivation
Strength	Encouragement
Character	Collaboration
Willpower	Self-determination
Success or failure	Celebration or commiseration
Doing	Thinking or feeling
Ignoring the difficulty	Being mindful of the difficulty
Determination	Reflection
Effort	Support
Enjoying reaching the goal	Enjoying the journey
Self-criticism	Self-care

In summary, rewards can traditionally be used in a way that, for developmentally traumatized children, can breed a kind of hopelessness, a sense of instant anticipation of failure and shame. But they can also be used in an inspiring, supportive, motivational and hopeful way that enables children impacted by abuse and/or neglect to overcome their expectation of failure and feel hopeful about their own mastery of the world and their ability to connect and achieve.

STRUCTURE AND ROUTINE

Introduction

Keeping things organized, knowing what comes next and clarity of expectations – these are things that come from maintaining structure and routine. Some of us default to this way of being in our lives as a whole and in our way of parenting, whilst for others, spontaneity and flexibility are more comfortable ways of being. In this chapter we will look beneath the surface of structure and routine in our parenting and how it can be unhelpfully and helpfully used.

Structure and routine in traditional reward–punishment parenting

In traditional reward–punishment parenting it is incredibly useful to maintain structure and routine. Typically, this is associated with consistency (in applying rules and consequences), predictability (knowing what will happen if a rule is broken) and finally, follow-through (enforcing the consequence, 'Say what you mean and mean what you say').

Structure and routine help with all of these things because they convey a sense of solidity and knowing where you stand. They enable a parent to be unambiguous in their expectations of their child. If structure and routine work for you and your child using this mindset, then that is truly wonderful. It can create calm and positivity in your relationship, and stability for you all. However, for many children who have experienced abuse and/or neglect, the emphasis on rules, consequences, power, dominance and compliance can be very difficult and creates more behavioural and relational challenges than it solves. Behaviourally focused structure and routine can be a near-constant reminder, for these children, of the abusive parental power that they have previously been traumatized by.

Structure and routine in EBM

In EBM we make use of structure and routine from an emotional containment perspective. Our focus is on decreasing anxiety rather than increasing conformity. To decrease anxiety, we empathically deploy familiarity and predictability. Creating environments (including relationships) that minimize stress by removing ambiguity and unpredictability can be hugely beneficial when coming from an empathic, 'mind-minded' position; for example, we might have a predictable bedtime routine because we know bedtimes are a scary time for our child.

Using reward–punishment thinking, structure and routine are primarily used to shape and manage behaviour. Using EBM, we are focused on trying to create security and safety and managing emotions. The nature of that structure and routine will change from day to day depending on the needs a child is expressing, but also as children grow and progress to greater levels of maturity and independence. When we have created this environment, constructive, connected and pro-social behaviour tends to follow.

How to create an environment of structure and routine from an empathic (EBM) perspective whilst avoiding the pitfalls of a behavioural containment mindset (reward–punishment) is laid out below.

✸ MACKENZIE AND RHONA

Mackenzie is 8 years old and lives with his adoptive mum, Rhona. Mackenzie is generally quite angry and defiant at home. He shouts at his mum whenever she makes any demands of him. Even the simplest things, like sitting down to eat dinner or going upstairs to bed result in

Mackenzie shouting and swearing at Rhona. He doesn't do this so much at school, and struggles with the changes to his routine during school holidays. Rhona has never been much of a fan of strict routines; she prefers to be responsive to what is going on at home and she works shifts in a supermarket, so life just has to be flexible.

Note: It is important to point out here that I am most certainly not implying, by my inclusion of this type of problem in this chapter, that they are always or even commonly 'fixed' by introducing more structure and routine, as this kind of presentation can be very complex. I am simply using this scenario as a way of exploring the impact of structure and routine from different approaches.

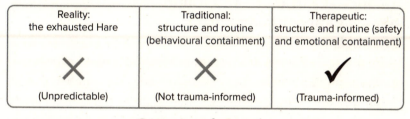

Reality: the exhausted Hare	Traditional: structure and routine (behavioural containment)	Therapeutic: structure and routine (safety and emotional containment)
✗	✗	✓
(Unpredictable)	(Not trauma-informed)	(Trauma-informed)

Comparison of approaches

Reality: the exhausted Hare
Approach
Rhona has developed a very understandable habit of trying to avoid Mackenzie's verbal aggression by making few demands of him. The two of them get on well most of the time, but Rhona reports that when there is a potential for conflict, she often finds herself trying to placate him and keep him happy. This results in keeping out of his way a great deal and leaving him to his own devices, such as watching TV or playing on his tablet.

Techniques
In relation to structure and routine, Rhona has taken to avoiding the demands that having a routine would necessitate, as she wants to get on well with her son and doesn't want to cause them to fall out. Rhona minimizes the demands she places on Mackenzie, and when she does

have to get things done, like bedtime or washing, etc., she has found that Mackenzie has started to sometimes do his bit if she agrees to give him something: 'I'll go to bed as long as I can take my tablet to bed' or 'I'll eat as long as I can eat in my room'. On the one hand, this could be seen as a flexible, responsive way of dealing with Mackenzie and his struggles in relationships. However, Rhona feels like she has lost all control and that she is no longer 'the parent'. She has also found herself feeling almost continually irritated with him and resentful about his control in their home. She sees how well Mackenzie does at school and feels more routine would help them both.

Traditional: structure and routine (behavioural containment)

Approach

There are several ways of understanding Mackenzie and Rhona's situation and the troubles they're experiencing. Any number of other things might be going on. However, in this chapter, we are exploring when structure and routine can be therapeutically and empathically used, and comparing that with when they can be used in a way that is neither therapeutic nor necessarily empathic. Therefore, in this section we will think about how a reward–punishment approach to structure and routine could be applied.

Using structure and routine in this way, Rhona would think about how to assert herself using the power she has over the rewards and punishments at her disposal.

Rhona's focus would be on changing Mackenzie's behaviour and manoeuvring them both into a position whereby Mackenzie doing desirable things at home has more beneficial consequences than doing things that make daily life more difficult.

Techniques

- Rhona may sit down with Mackenzie in a calm moment and work with him to develop a routine, talking to him about why she feels it's important for them both (this could certainly be part of an empathic approach too). Alternatively, Rhona may do this alone, but she would typically work with Mackenzie to decide what they will do and in what order.

- Rhona may emphasize Mackenzie's responsibility to stick to the routine and behave 'well', with Rhona's own responsibility likely to be centred on having failed to be strong enough to uphold structure and routine.
- The two of them would work out what reasonable expectations of Mackenzie would be, or Rhona may do this alone – they should be kept simple and achievable and written down into a written or pictorial routine.
- Rhona and Mackenzie would also work out what Mackenzie would be rewarded with, and/or what the consequences may be for him of not sticking to what they agree.
- Rhona's responsibility would be to stick to the schedule and to apply the rewards and consequences. Mackenzie's responsibility would be to do his best to behave 'well' (in accordance with the routine either agreed on or that which Rhona decides is important).

Therapeutic: structure and routine (safety and emotional containment)

Approach

Taking a therapeutic, empathic approach, Rhona would be encouraged to begin with reflecting on how difficult all of this has been for her. The aim here is for Rhona to give herself credit for the toll Mackenzie's anger and hostility has taken on her and to enable her to see what support she might need to enable her to cope into the future. This serves a dual purpose – to support Rhona in her own right, but also to help her to consider the personal demands that parenting therapeutically will make on her, and so enable her to engage in this in a better-informed and better-equipped way. This, in no way, places blame or responsibility with Rhona, but simply allows an objectively empathic way of understanding Rhona and Mackenzie's relationship and the things that might make it work better and be more sustainable.

Structure and routine from an empathic stance would require us to look closely at the emotional stability that they offer and how trauma may be impacting Mackenzie emotionally (and therefore behaviourally). Structure and routine can very often provide a sense of stability, predictability and reliability that form the basis of environmental and relational safety for children who may have experienced a traumatic absence or abusive experience of adults. Introducing such things can be tremendously therapeutic, even though in many cases children will react against the imposition of something (even consensually) as this means an adult will be in control. Their experience of such things may be permeated with abusive memories and understandings of adult authority.

Techniques

- Rhona would be encouraged to find a support network that would allow her to speak freely and without judgement about her struggles with Mackenzie, and also with someone who will not undermine any attempt Rhona is making to parent therapeutically by judging the way she would like to parent or by bringing their own agenda or view on how she 'should' be doing things. The goal for Rhona would be to help her to feel more regulated and less subject to the pressure she feels to 'back off' in her parenting. She would be helped to 'raise her presence' in the household, so that she could feel safely in control for Mackenzie (and herself).
- Rhona could explore by herself and/or with a trusted friend or professional why she wants to start thinking about introducing more structure and routine, and why doing this has been difficult for her in the past.
- Rhona could sit down with Mackenzie at a calm time to talk about why sticking to a schedule is difficult for them both. She would be actively curious about Mackenzie's thoughts and experiences of structure and routine. Rhona might wonder with him whether Mackenzie struggles with her being in control because of what he has experienced in his past. She

might also wonder aloud whether it might make him feel safer because he will know what to expect.

- They would collaborate in devising a schedule and Rhona would find some genuine acceptance of things that may not be her preference, but she will also be assertive and in control *for* (see Superpower #2: Safe Containment) about anything she thinks would not be in Mackenzie's (or her) best interests.
- Rhona would model routine and structure as best she could.
- She would accept when she and Mackenzie struggle with the routine, but would not dwell on it, and just get back to it as soon as they can.
- There wouldn't necessarily be any rewards for sticking to the routine, or consequences for struggling to stick with it (unless there was a clear empathically developed understanding that this would help with motivation and/or hope) (see Superpower #9: Building Motivation and Hope).

Let's get practical
Parents' relationship with structure and routine

As always, when thinking about the therapeutic benefit of structure and routine, we start with ourselves. It's worth thinking carefully about how you feel about structure and routine and what you associate with it. In essence, you are helping yourself to understand why it hasn't happened before.

What do structure and routine mean to you?

Try asking yourself the following questions:

1. What are structure and routine? What do they look like in other people's homes?
2. What is your personal experience of structure and routine?
   a. When you were a child?
   b. In your previous parenting experience?
3. What words do you associate with structure and routine?
4. What feelings do you associate with structure and routine?
5. What is your relationship with structure and routine?

6. If it's not a positive one, what could you do to help your relationship with structure and routine?

The 'why now?' conversation

The next step is to be honest with yourself about the advantages and disadvantages of introducing routine and structure in your family, perhaps even writing the pros and cons in two columns. More than simply a list, going through this process will help you to accept, without shame, those things in your relationship with structure and routine that you may judge yourself for. Using this list you can also work out why structure and routine need to change now, whether now is the right time for you, and whether the pros now outweigh the cons.

Planning, preparation and troubleshooting

The next exercise to take this to a more practical level would be to ask yourself and your child the following questions:

1. What will it feel like when we stick to the routine even when you/your child don't feel like it? What support will you/your child need when it gets tough?
2. How will you prevent the therapeutic use of structure and routine becoming reward–punishment based?
3. How will you maximize your chances of keeping annoyance, anger and irritation out of maintaining your structure and routine?
4. How will you minimize your chances of giving up on structure and routine?
5. What will be hard about it?
6. What might deter you in reality?
7. How will life feel different for you and your child when there is greater structure and routine?
8. When have you managed to maintain more structure or routine in the past? What supported you to do this?

Naming without blaming or shaming

It's important when talking to our children about introducing structure and routine that we talk honestly about what the problems are in a straightforward and accepting way. Avoiding the truth of difficulties simply conveys that those parts of a child are unacceptable to us.

There are certain golden rules for naming without blaming or shaming:

- Problems are there for a reason.
- Problems exist in the space between you and your child rather than 'in' your child or 'in' you.
- Problems need to be acknowledged in order to minimize the shame associated with them.
- Ignoring problems increases shame by making those parts of your relationship with your child feel 'unacceptable'.
- The solutions exist in the space between you and your child.
- You, as the parent or carer, will take a lead in working on the problems – in this case, being in control *for* your child (not in control *of* them), and making sure the structure and routine happen, even when it's hard.

Examples of naming without shaming include:

- 'It's a huge struggle for you to stick to the things we've agreed, isn't it. I get it, and I'm sorry it's so hard! I'm going to try and help in any way I can.'
- 'I get that brushing your teeth feels difficult. I haven't quite worked out why yet, but I want to help in any way I can.'
- 'We fall out so much when we have to get jobs done in the evening, don't we?! You get cross with me for asking you to eat your dinner and I get grumpy and snappy with you. That's no good for us! I'm going to work out some ideas about how to make this better.'
- 'Life just feels a bit all over the place in our house at the moment and I want to help your head feel calmer and safer, so I'm going to try and help us get organized.'

Visual schedules

Transparency and clarity are incredibly important in therapeutically applying structure and routine. This enables your children to take (at least partial) ownership of the process, which can undercut the issues that traumatized children often have with an adult taking control in any way.

Visual schedules are a great way of establishing an objective independent source of understanding regarding structure and routine. This technique could well be used when taking a reward–punishment approach but, of course, we rely on empathy, understanding and acceptance in this case, rather than willpower and self-discipline.

You and your child can sit down together and decide on the important things that need to be achieved in a day – this is a collaborative approach, but in order to provide safety and emotional containment for your child, you may need to insist that some things are included when they are really necessary, such as getting dressed for school, brushing teeth, etc. Before you get to this stage, you must ensure that you have fully understood why your child is resistant to these things.

You can then tailor the next stage to suit the age of your child. You can define a morning routine and an evening routine, or whatever it is that you're struggling with. It's helpful to find pictures together to represent each job that needs doing, making sure they suit the age of your child, and then agree a time frame or at least an order in which the jobs should happen.

You may need a different schedule for weekends and school holidays.

In order to give your child greater control of the schedule day to day, you could adapt it by agreeing on a set of jobs that need doing but then your child can choose which order they happen each day. You could use a laminated sheet with a Velcro® strip on it and then attach Velcro® or Blu Tack® tabs to the back of each pictured task.

Joint ownership

Another way of increasing engagement in new routines is to display written or pictorial information in multiple neutral places, such as on the fridge, bathroom door, etc. Then, when it comes to using the routine, you can ask your child to be in charge and tell you what comes next if they are struggling without a reminder.

Monitoring the impact

It is often helpful when introducing any new strategy with your child to jointly evaluate how well it is working after you've been trying it for a while. This facilitates shared ownership and contributes to the therapeutic, empathic approach. It conveys a sense that you will not be taking an uncompromising, authoritarian approach in your relationship or in relation to your use of structure and routine. This, as with all of our therapeutic approaches to structure and routine, has the ultimate aim of creating greater safety and emotional containment for our children, and thus enabling behavioural containment to follow.

CONCLUSION

So how are you doing? How was reading the book?

I know you can't really talk to me, so I'll have a guess...

'I'm excited and energized! I'm raring to get going, but also a bit daunted at how different it all seems – I think I'm going to get it wrong sometimes...'

Fabulous! That's great news! I'm so pleased this book struck a chord for you. That's really all you need to start with. There's pretty much only one promise I can make and that is, you're right, you will struggle with this stuff sometimes. I do too. But really, that's the point. If it wasn't challenging, it would mean it wasn't different enough to make a difference! We all default to our old ways of doing things, that's our impulsive Hare system at work.

The great news, is that noticing when we're doing things in a way we don't want to, and then correcting that through repair, is another way of being a 'superparent'. When we do this we are showing huge understanding and acceptance of our inner worlds and those of our children. For example, saying 'I'm sorry sweetheart, I shouted earlier when you needed me to understand what was going on for you' helps them in at least two different ways. It enables you to repair your relationship with your child AND it models to them that even when they behave impulsively, unkindly or without empathy they can still put it right. They may even apologize to you one day!

Relationship repair is something I have talked about in almost every chapter (for a good starting place, see Superpower #2: Safe

Containment). It really is the most magically soothing balm for relationships. It can seem laden with guilt and shame as we feel we have let ourselves and/or our child down, but it really needn't be. We will all need to repair at times when things have gone wrong; it's inevitable. It can provide a heart-swelling, joyous moments of reconnection.

If you're feeling worried about getting things 'wrong', please go back to our first superpower, without which nothing works, and practice some self-acceptance. Know that you're okay, you're doing your best in tough circumstances, you're trying, or you want to try, and that's good enough. YOU are good enough.

> 'It was tough going to be honest, Amber. I haven't read the book cover to cover. I've picked it up and put it down in amongst being busy doing other things. It's going to take me a while to digest it all.'

Of course it is! You've got such a huge amount on your plate! You've picked this book up because you need some support, not because life was going swimmingly. Give yourself a break, let it sink in, and come back to it if you need to.

For those of you feeling a bit beaten down by life at the moment and those who are struggling to digest anything new, let me narrow it down for you a bit. Start by looking at our first superpower chapter and read about self-acceptance. I promise that everything else will come from there. Read it on a loop if you need to. This chapter will help you to be gentle with yourself. If you're doing that you won't be able to stop yourself from modelling that to your child(ren). They will learn from you that inner worlds matter, that they all deserve nurture. Your children will see that impulses take control sometimes, but that as long as we see and acknowledge this fact, and we are kind enough to free ourselves from shame, there is a way out to do things differently.

Good luck and take care!

Amber

Glossary

Attunement describes how reactive a person is to another's emotional needs and moods. A person who is well attuned will respond with appropriate language and behaviours based on another person's emotional state. It is linked to empathy, that is, the ability to read and feel another person's emotional state.

Blocked care (or parenting) is a state parents can enter when prolonged stress suppresses their capacity to sustain loving and empathic feelings towards their child.

Countercontrol is a response to aversive control. The individual who is exposed to aversive control may try to oppose controlling attempts through the process of negative reinforcement, such as by escaping, attacking or passively resisting. In parent–child interactions marked by control and countercontrol, it can become unclear who is in ultimate control of the situation. Parents often feel like they are 'treading on eggshells'.

Dissociation is a way the mind copes with too much stress. It can make people feel disconnected from themselves and the world around them. It can cause people to forget a period of time and a feeling that you are unsure of who you are.

Dyadic Developmental Psychotherapy (DDP) is a therapy based on the potential of healthy, therapeutic parenting relationships to heal relational trauma.

Dysregulation, also known as emotional dysregulation, refers to a poor ability to manage emotional responses or to keep them within an acceptable range of typical emotional reactions. This can refer to a wide range of emotions, including sadness, anger, irritability and frustration.

Empathic Behaviour Management (EBM) is a relationship and emotion-based approach to supporting children who may have experienced developmental trauma. It focuses on the internal experiences of children and young people.

Intersubjectivity is the shared, reciprocal, experience between parent and child whereby the experience of each is having an impact on the experience of the other. For example, children experience themselves as being loved, lovable, valued, valuable and clever whenever their parents experience them as manifesting those characteristics.

Neuropsychology is a branch of psychology that is concerned with how the brain and the rest of the nervous system influence a person's cognition and behaviours.

Non-Violent Resistance (NVR) is a form of therapeutic intervention, which has been developed for aggressive, violent, controlling and self-destructive behaviour in young people.

Social learning theory is a school of thought first proposed by Albert Bandura. The basis of the theory is that people learn best from watching other people doing things. In the context of parenting programmes, social learning theory is typically accompanied by behavioural theory and it is therefore paired with rewards, consequences, ignoring 'bad' behaviour, and star charts, amongst other things.

Toxic stress response can occur when a child experiences strong, frequent and/or prolonged adversity, such as physical or emotional abuse, chronic neglect, caregiver substance abuse or mental illness, exposure to violence and/or the accumulated burdens of family economic hardship, without adequate adult support.

Endnotes

1   Skinner, B.F. (2009) 'About behaviorism (1974).' In B.F. Gentile and B.O. Miller (eds) *Foundations of Psychological Thought: A History of Psychology*. Thousand Oaks, CA: SAGE Publishing.

2   Skinner, B.F. (1971) *Beyond Freedom and Dignity*. New York, NY: Alfred A. Knopf.

3   Skinner, B.F. (1948) *Walden Two*. Indianapolis, IN: Hackett Publishing Co.

4   See www.smithsonianmag.com/science-nature/bf-skinner-the-man-who-taught-pigeons-to-play-ping-pong-and-rats-to-pull-levers-5363946

5   Skinner, B.F. (1948) *Walden Two*. Indianapolis, IN: Hackett Publishing Co.

6   De Wolff, M.S. and van Ijzendoorn, M.H. (1997) 'Sensitivity and attachment: A meta-analysis on parental antecedents of infant attachment.' *Child Development 68*, 4, 571–591.

7   Nachmias, M., Gunnar, M., Mangelsdorf, S., Parritz, R.H. and Buss, K. (1996) 'Behavioral inhibition and stress reactivity: The moderating role of attachment security.' *Child Development 67*, 2, 508–522.

8   See www.cdc.gov/violenceprevention/aces/index.html

9   www.cdc.gov/violenceprevention/aces/fastfact.html?CDC_AA_refVal=https%3A%2F%2Fwww.cdc.gov%2Fviolenceprevention%2Facestudy%2Ffastfact.html

10 Dube, S.R., Fairweather, D., Pearson, W.S., Felitti, V.J., Anda, R.F. and Croft, J.B. (2009) 'Cumulative childhood stress and autoimmune diseases in adults.' *Psychosomatic Medicine 71*, 2, 243.

11 Strine, T.W., Dube, S.R., Edwards, V.J., Prehn, A.W., *et al.* (2012) 'Associations between adverse childhood experiences, psychological distress, and adult alcohol problems.' *American Journal of Health Behavior 36*, 3, 408–423.

12 Ports, K.A., Holman, D.M., Guinn, A.S., Pampati, S., *et al.* (2019) 'Adverse childhood experiences and the presence of cancer risk factors in adulthood: A scoping review of the literature from 2005 to 2015.' *Journal of Pediatric Nursing 44*, 81–96.

13 De Wolff, M.S. and van Ijzendoorn, M.H. (1997) 'Sensitivity and attachment: A meta-analysis on parental antecedents of infant attachment.' *Child Development 68*, 4, 571–591.

14 Liston, C., Miller, M.M., Goldwater, D.S., Radley, J.J., *et al.* (2006) 'Stress-induced alterations in prefrontal cortical dendritic morphology predict selective impairments in perceptual attentional set-shifting.' *Journal of Neuroscience 26*, 30, 7870–7874.

15 Liston, C., McEwen, B.S. and Casey, B.J. (2009) 'Psychosocial stress reversibly disrupts prefrontal processing and attentional control.' *Proceedings of the National Academy of Sciences 106*, 3, 912–917.

16 Nachmias, M., Gunnar, M., Mangelsdorf, S., Parritz, R.H. and Buss, K. (1996) 'Behavioral inhibition and stress reactivity: The moderating role of attachment security.' *Child Development 67*, 2, 508–522.

17 Sapolsky, R.M., Romero, L.M. and Munck, A.U. (2000) 'How do glucocorticoids influence stress responses? Integrating permissive, suppressive, stimulatory, and preparative actions.' *Endocrine Reviews 21*, 1, 55–89.

18 Lupien, S.J., de Leon, M., De Santi, S., Convit, A., *et al.* (1998) 'Cortisol levels during human aging predict hippocampal atrophy and memory deficits.' *Nature Neuroscience 1*, 1, 69–73.

19 Lupien, S.J., McEwen, B.S., Gunnar, M.R. and Heim, C. (2009) 'Effects of stress throughout the lifespan on the brain, behaviour and cognition.' *Nature Reviews Neuroscience 10*, 6, 434–445.

20 Brunson, K.L., Grigoriadis, D.E., Lorang, M.T. and Baram, T.Z. (2002) 'Corticotropin-releasing hormone (CRH) downregulates the function of its receptor (CRF1) and induces CRF1 expression in hippocampal and cortical regions of the immature rat brain.' *Experimental Neurology 176*, 1, 75–86.

21 Liston, C., McEwen, B.S. and Casey, B.J. (2009) 'Psychosocial stress reversibly disrupts prefrontal processing and attentional control.' *Proceedings of the National Academy of Sciences 106*, 3, 912–917.

22 Goldsmith, D.F. and Rogoff, B. (1997) 'Mothers' and toddlers' coordinated joint focus of attention: Variations with maternal dysphoric symptoms.' *Developmental Psychology 33*, 1, 113.

23 Kochanska, G. and Knaack, A. (2003) 'Effortful control as a personality characteristic of young children: Antecedents, correlates, and consequences.' *Journal of Personality, 71*, 6, 1087–1112.

24 Lengua, L.J., Honorado, E. and Bush, N.R. (2007) 'Contextual risk and parenting as predictors of effortful control and social competence in preschool children.' *Journal of Applied Developmental Psychology 28*, 1, 40–55.

25 Maughan, A. and Cicchetti, D. (2002) 'Impact of child maltreatment and interadult violence on children's emotion regulation abilities and socioemotional adjustment.' *Child Development 73*, 5, 1525–1542.

26 O'Connor, T.G., Rutter, M. and English and Romanian Adoptees Study Team (2000) 'Attachment disorder behavior following early severe deprivation: Extension and longitudinal follow-up.' *Journal of the American Academy of Child & Adolescent Psychiatry 39*, 6, 703–712.

27 Pollak, S., Cicchetti, D. and Klorman, R. (1998) 'Stress, memory, and emotion: Developmental considerations from the study of child maltreatment.' *Development and Psychopathology 10*, 4, 811–828.

28 Sanchez, M.M., Ladd, C.O. and Plotsky, P.M. (2001) 'Early adverse experience as a developmental risk factor for later psychopathology: Evidence from rodent and primate models.' *Development and Psychopathology 13*, 3, 419–449.

29 Kochanska, G., Murray, K. and Coy, K.C. (1997) 'Inhibitory control as a contributor to conscience in childhood: From toddler to early school age.' *Child Development 68*, 2, 263–277.

30 Blair, C. and Diamond, A. (2008) 'Biological processes in prevention and intervention: The promotion of self-regulation as a means of preventing school failure.' *Development and Psychopathology 20*, 3, 899.

31 Kochanska, G., Murray, K., Jacques, T.Y., Koenig, A.L. and Vandegeest, K.A. (1996) 'Inhibitory control in young children and its role in emerging internalization.' *Child Development 67*, 2, 490–507.

32 Blair, C. (2002) 'School readiness: Integrating cognition and emotion in a neurobiological conceptualization of children's functioning at school entry.' *American Psychologist 57*, 2, 111.

33 Bodrova, E., Germeroth, C. and Leong, D.J. (2013) 'Play and self-regulation: Lessons from Vygotsky.' *American Journal of Play 6*, 1, 111–123.

34 Elliott, A. (2013) *Why Can't My Child Behave? Empathic Parenting Strategies that Work for Adoptive and Foster Families.* London: Jessica Kingsley Publishers.

35 Kahneman, D. (2011) *Thinking, Fast and Slow.* Basingstoke: Macmillan.

36 Hughes, D.A. and Golding, K. (2012) *Creating Loving Attachments: Parenting with PACE to Nurture Confidence and Security in the Troubled Child.* London: Jessica Kingsley Publishers.

37 Hughes, D.A. and Baylin, J. (2012) *Brain-Based Parenting: The Neuroscience of Caregiving for Healthy Attachment* (Norton Series on Interpersonal Neurobiology). New York, NY: W.W. Norton & Co.

38 Jakob, P. (2011) *Re-Connecting Parents and Young People with Serious Behaviour Problems: Child-Focused Practice and Reconciliation Work in Non Violent Resistance Therapy.* Cambridge: New Authority Network International.

39 Hughes, D.A. and Baylin, J. (2012) *Brain-Based Parenting: The Neuroscience of Caregiving for Healthy Attachment* (Norton Series on Interpersonal Neurobiology). New York, NY: W.W. Norton & Co.

40 Porges, S.W. (2007) 'The polyvagal perspective.' *Biological Psychology 74*, 2, 116–143.

41 Porges, S.W. (2009) 'The polyvagal theory: New insights into adaptive reactions of the autonomic nervous system.' *Cleveland Clinic Journal of Medicine 76*, Suppl. 2, S86.

42 Jakob, P. (2011) *Re-Connecting Parents and Young People with Serious Behaviour Problems: Child-Focused Practice and Reconciliation Work in Non Violent Resistance Therapy.* Cambridge: New Authority Network International.

43 Porges, S.W. (2007) 'The polyvagal perspective.' *Biological Psychology 74*, 2, 116–143.

44 Porges, S.W. (2009) 'The polyvagal theory: New insights into adaptive reactions of the autonomic nervous system.' *Cleveland Clinic Journal of Medicine 76*, Suppl. 2, S86.

45 Siegel, D.J. and Hartzell, M. (2013) *Parenting from the Inside Out: How a Deeper Self-Understanding Can Help You Raise Children Who Thrive.* London: Penguin.

46 Golding, K. (2017) Everyday *Parenting with Security and Love: Using PACE to Provide Foundations for Attachment.* London: Jessica Kingsley Publishers.

47 Hughes, D.A. and Golding, K. (2012) *Creating Loving Attachments: Parenting with PACE to Nurture Confidence and Security in the Troubled Child.* London: Jessica Kingsley Publishers.

48 Hughes, D.A. (2004) 'An attachment-based treatment of maltreated children and young people.' *Attachment & Human Development 6*, 3, 263–278.

49 Golding, K. (2017) *Everyday Parenting with Security and Love: Using PACE to Provide Foundations for Attachment.* London: Jessica Kingsley Publishers.

50 Hughes, D.A. and Golding, K. (2012) *Creating Loving Attachments: Parenting with PACE to Nurture Confidence and Security in the Troubled Child.* London: Jessica Kingsley Publishers.

51 Hughes, D.A. (2004) 'An attachment-based treatment of maltreated children and young people.' *Attachment & Human Development 6*, 3, 263–278.

52 Hughes, D.A. and Golding, K. (2012) *Creating Loving Attachments: Parenting with PACE to Nurture Confidence and Security in the Troubled Child.* London: Jessica Kingsley Publishers.

53 Golding, K. (2017) *Everyday Parenting with Security and Love: Using PACE to Provide Foundations for Attachment.* London: Jessica Kingsley Publishers.

54 Hughes, D.A. and Golding, K. (2012) *Creating Loving Attachments: Parenting with PACE to Nurture Confidence and Security in the Troubled Child.* London: Jessica Kingsley Publishers.

55 Hughes, D.A. (2004) 'An attachment-based treatment of maltreated children and young people.' *Attachment & Human Development 6*, 3, 263–278.

56   Golding, K. (2017) *Everyday Parenting with Security and Love: Using PACE to Provide Foundations for Attachment*. London: Jessica Kingsley Publishers.

57   See https://ddpnetwork.org/about-ddp/meant-pace/

58   Chiesa, M. and Fonagy, P. (2014) 'Reflective function as a mediator between childhood adversity, personality disorder and symptom distress.' *Personality and Mental Health* 8, 1, 52–66.

59   www.headspace.com

60   www.calm.com/?gclid=CjwKCAiAi_D_BRApEiwASslbJ-aezcraSwrpVoylPocRd7o WhznOrWflDr-nma5r_vJdXBkC8ejpEhoCtDoQAvD_BwE

61   Jakob, P. (2011) *Re-Connecting Parents and Young People with Serious Behaviour Problems: Child-Focused Practice and Reconciliation Work in Non Violent Resistance Therapy*. Cambridge: New Authority Network International.

62   Donovan, S. (2013) *No Matter What: An Adoptive Family's Story of Hope, Love and Healing*. London: Jessica Kingsley Publishers.

63   Donovan, S. (2014) *The Unofficial Guide to Adoptive Parenting: The Small Stuff, the Big Stuff and the Stuff in Between*. London: Jessica Kingsley Publishers.

64   Kuypers, L. (2011) *The Zones of Regulation*. San Jose, CA: Think Social Publishing.

65   Kuypers, L. (2011) *The Zones of Regulation*. San Jose, CA: Think Social Publishing.

66   Siegel, D.J. (1999) *The Developing Mind: Toward a Neurobiology of Interpersonal Experience*. New York, NY: Guilford Press.

67   Jakob, P. (2011) *Re-Connecting Parents and Young People with Serious Behaviour Problems: Child-Focused Practice and Reconciliation Work in Non Violent Resistance Therapy*. Cambridge: New Authority Network International.

Index